Laboratory Manual of Soil Science

Syeda & Syed

SPI Publications

Published by SPI Publications, www.spipublications.in
SPI, the SPI logo, and Split Poetry India are trademarks of SPI Publications, or its affiliates.
ISBN-13: 978-93-49860-04-9

First Edition 2025

SPI Publications

Corporate & Editorial Office

117/2, Sector 37, Khandsa Road,
Gurgaon, Haryana 122 001
Phone: +91 98355 52940
Email: contact@spipublications.in
Website: www.spipublications.in

Processed and Printed in India

ABOUT THE AUTHORS

Syeda Nahal Zahra Rizvi is a dedicated scholar and researcher in the field of Environmental Sciences from Sher-e-Kashmir University of Agricultural Sciences and Technology of Kashmir (SKUAST-K), with a strong academic background in Agriculture and Soil Science, she has consistently demonstrated excellence in both theoretical knowledge and practical application. With hands-on experience in soil sampling, analysis, and sustainable soil management techniques, the author has contributed significantly to the academic and research community. Their expertise particularly spans biochar technology, soil carbon sequestration, and integrated waste management, reflecting their commitment to addressing pressing environmental challenges. They have authored and co-authored several peer-reviewed papers and articles on topics such as climate change, modern environmental disasters, urban dumping site impacts, light pollution, and the ill effects of pesticide residues on soil and microbial health. These contributions have appeared in respected journals and environmental science forums. Beyond academics, the author is also a two-time national gold medallist in roller netted ball, showcasing an exceptional balance between intellectual pursuits and athletic excellence.

Syed Touba Qureshi is a postgraduate in Entomology from Sher-e-Kashmir University of Agricultural Sciences and Technology of Kashmir (SKUAST-K). While her academic foundation lies in the study of insects, her broader passion encompasses sustainable agriculture and soil health. This interdisciplinary interest has led her to develop this soil science laboratory manual, aiming to bridge the gap between entomological insights and soil science applications. Her academic journey reflects a commitment to understanding the intricate relationships between soil ecosystems and agricultural productivity. By integrating knowledge from entomology and soil science, she seeks to provide students and researchers with practical methodologies that enhance soil fertility and promote sustainable farming practices. Beyond her academic pursuits, the author is dedicated to contributing to the agricultural sector by developing region-specific strategies that address local challenges. Her work emphasizes the importance of soil health in achieving food security and environmental sustainability.

This laboratory manual stands as a testament to the authors' dedication to advancing agricultural education and promoting interdisciplinary scientific inquiry. By combining both their expertise in entomology and environmental sciences with a deep interest in soil science, their vision is to provide a comprehensive, practical, and student-friendly guide for learners, researchers, and professionals in Soil Science and allied fields.

PREFACE

Soil science is a multidisciplinary field that lies at the intersection of agriculture, ecology, and environmental stewardship. As graduates in Agriculture with specialisations in Environmental Sciences and Entomology respectively, we have always recognised soil not just as a medium for plant growth, but as a living, dynamic system integral to sustaining life, regulating climate, and supporting biodiversity.

This Soil Science Laboratory Manual has been developed with a vision to bridge classroom concepts with hands-on experimentation. The manual brings together a diverse range of practicals—from fundamental analyses like pH, texture, and nutrient status, to advanced investigations into soil microbial biomass, pesticide impact, biochar application, and carbon sequestration.

Our aim is to offer students, especially undergraduates and postgraduates in Agriculture and Environmental Studies, a comprehensive and practical resource that is aligned with current academic standards, while also incorporating sustainability-oriented and research-driven practices.

Drawing from our respective disciplines, this manual explores soil from multiple lenses—how contaminants influence microbial diversity, how organic practices like vermicomposting enrich fertility, and how insects and micro-fauna play key roles in soil health. We have ensured that each experiment is structured with a clear principle, a detailed procedure, observation formats, and relevant precautions and references.We hope this manual not only equips students with essential laboratory skills but also fosters a broader understanding of soil as a critical environmental component—worthy of research, respect, and responsible management.

We are grateful to our university, faculty mentors, and most importantly, our families and the Almighty for their continuous support and encouragement throughout this journey.

— ***The Authors***

TABLE OF CONTENTS

Module 1

Module 2

Module 3

Module 4

Module 5

Annexures

Module 1

Basics of Soil Science

Experiment 01

Determination of Soil Texture (By Hydrometer and Feel Method).

Principle

The *hydrometer method* is based on ***Stokes' Law,*** which states that particles settle at different rates in a liquid depending on their size, shape, and density. By measuring the density of the suspension at specific time intervals with a hydrometer, we can estimate the percentages of sand, silt, and clay in a soil sample. The *feel method* is a qualitative approach where soil is moistened and worked by hand to estimate its textural class based on grittiness, stickiness, and plasticity.

Part A: Hydrometer Method

Materials Required

Soil sample (air-dried and sieved), 1000 ml measuring cylinder (sedimentation cylinder), Hydrometer (Bouyoucos type), Mechanical stirrer or blender, Sodium hexametaphosphate (dispersing agent) – 5%, Distilled water, Thermometer, Stopper, Balance (accurate to 0.01 g), Watch or stopwatch.

Procedure

1. **Sample Preparation:**
   - Weigh 50 g of air-dried, sieved soil (<2 mm).
   - Add it to a beaker containing 100 ml of 5% sodium hexametaphosphate.
   - Allow to soak for 10–15 minutes.
2. **Dispersion:**
   - Stir the soil-dispersant mixture with a mechanical stirrer for 5–10 minutes.
3. **Transfer to Cylinder:**
   - Transfer the suspension to a 1000 ml graduated cylinder.
   - Add distilled water to make the volume up to 1000 ml.
   - Shake the cylinder vigorously for 1 minute and start the stopwatch immediately.
4. **Hydrometer Reading:**
   - Insert the hydrometer gently at 40 seconds and record the first reading (R_1).
   - After 2 hours, insert the hydrometer again and record the second reading (R_2).
   - Also, record the temperature at both times and apply temperature corrections if necessary.

Calculations:

Let:

- **R_1** = Hydrometer reading after 40 sec (represents suspension of silt + clay)
- **R_2** = Hydrometer reading after 2 hrs (represents clay)
- **W** = Oven dry weight of soil used (g)

Then,

- % **Sand** = $100 - (R_1/W) \times 100$
- % **Clay** = $(R_2/W) \times 100$
- % **Silt** = 100 – (% Sand + % Clay)

Use a soil textural triangle to determine the textural class.

Precautions:

- Ensure complete dispersion of soil particles.
- Avoid bubbles in hydrometer readings.
- Take hydrometer readings at eye level
- Account for temperature corrections if different from standard (20°C).

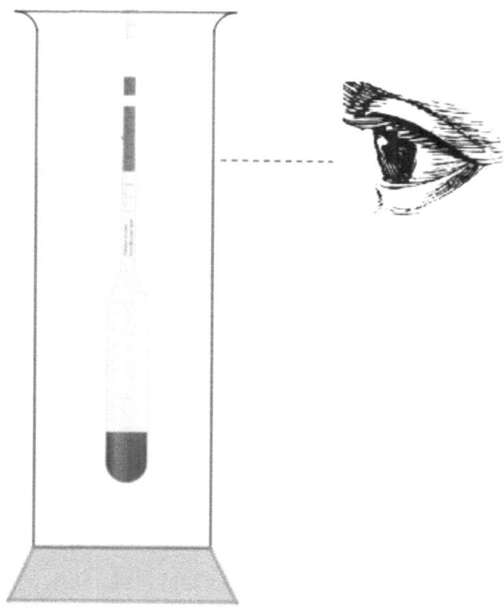

The Hydrometer is read by seeing the line where the liquid goes across the scale

Part B: Feel Method

Materials Required

Soil sample, Water, Porcelain plate or clean surface.

Procedure

- Moisten a small amount of soil slowly until it feels like putty (not sticky or runny).
- Roll it into a ball and then into a ribbon between thumb and forefinger.
- Observe:
    - Gritty feel indicates sand.
    - Smooth and floury feel indicates silt.
    - Sticky and plastic feel indicates clay.
- Based on the length of ribbon formed and texture, classify the soil as:
    - Sandy
    - Sandy loam
    - Loam
    - Silty loam
    - Clay loam
    - Clay, etc.

Advantages

- Quick and cost-effective
- Useful for field-level estimations

Result

Method	Sand (%)	Silt (%)	Clay (%)	Textural Class
Hydrometer	XX	XX	XX	e.g., Loam
Feel Method	-	-	-	e.g., Clay loam

Experiment 02

Soil Colour and Its Significance (Using Munsell Soil Colour Chart)

Principle

Soil colour serves as an important diagnostic feature in soil science, reflecting various physical and chemical characteristics. The Munsell Soil Colour System provides a standardized method to describe soil colour based on three components:

- **Hue**: The dominant spectral colour (e.g., 10YR, 5YR, 2.5YR).
- **Value**: The lightness or darkness of the colour, ranging from 0 (black) to 10 (white).
- **Chroma**: The intensity or purity of the colour, indicating the strength of the hue.

By matching soil samples to the Munsell colour chips, scientists can consistently describe and compare soil colours across different regions and studies.

Materials Required

Munsell Soil Colour Chart, Spade or soil auger, Clean white paper or ceramic plate, Distilled water (for moistening samples, if necessary), Notebook and pen/pencil for recording observations, Hand lens (optional, for detailed examination).

Procedure

1. **Sample Collection**:
   - Using a spade or soil auger, collect soil samples from the desired depth (typically 10–20 cm below the surface) to avoid surface contamination.
   - Place the sample on a clean white surface to provide a neutral background for colour comparison.
2. **Moisture Assessment**:
   - Determine whether to assess the soil colour in its moist or dry state. Moist soil often provides more consistent colour readings.
   - If the soil is dry and moist colour assessment is desired, add distilled water gradually until the soil reaches a moist consistency without being saturated.
3. **Colour Matching**:
   - Hold the Munsell Soil Colour Chart next to the soil sample under natural light conditions (preferably on a cloudy day or in shaded area to avoid glare).
   - Compare the soil sample to the colour chips in the chart, identifying the closest match in terms of hue, value, and chroma.
   - Record the Munsell notation (e.g., 10YR 5/3) along with the moisture condition of the sample.

For comprehensive analysis, repeat the colour determination for multiple samples from different locations or depths as required.

Observation

Sample ID	Depth (cm)	Moisture Condition	Munsell Notation	General Colour Description	Sample ID

Note: Fill in the table with the observed data for each soil sample.

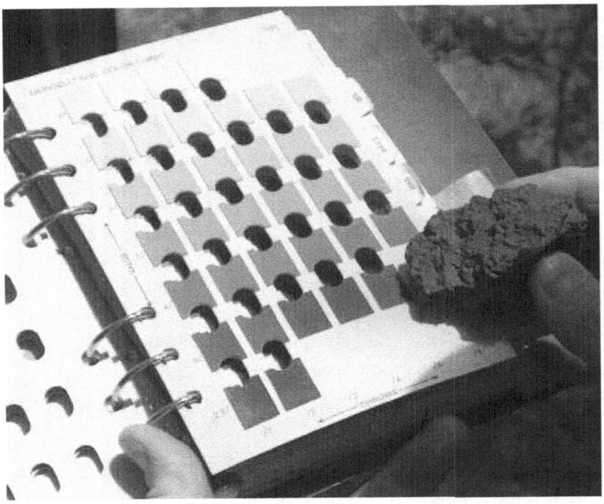

Comparing the soil sample colour against Munsell Soil Colour Chart

Precautions

- Ensure that soil samples are free from debris and organic matter that may alter colour perception.
- Avoid direct sunlight when comparing colours, as it can distort the appearance of both soil and colour chips.
- Do not touch the colour chips with wet or dirty hands to prevent staining.
- Always document the moisture condition of the soil, as colour can vary significantly between moist and dry states.

Significance

Soil colour provides valuable information about:

- **Organic Matter Content**: Darker soils often indicate higher organic matter.

- **Drainage Conditions**: Bright red or brown colours suggest well-drained soils, while grey or bluish hues may indicate poor drainage or waterlogged conditions.
- **Mineral Composition**: Specific colours can reflect the presence of certain minerals, such as iron oxides imparting reddish tones.

Understanding soil colour aids in soil classification, fertility assessment, and land-use planning.

Significance of Soil Colour

Colour	Likely Indication
Dark brown/black	High organic matter, good fertility
Red/yellow	Presence of iron oxides, well-drained, aerobic conditions
Grey/bluish	Poor drainage, waterlogging, anaerobic conditions
White/light	Presence of salts, lime or silica, low fertility

Experiment 03

Bulk Density and Particle Density Measurement

Principle

Bulk density is defined as the mass of oven-dry soil per unit volume, including the pore spaces. It is a critical parameter influencing root penetration, water movement, and soil aeration. The core method involves extracting a known volume of undisturbed soil using a cylindrical core sampler and determining its dry mass.

Particle density refers to the mass of soil solids per unit volume, excluding pore spaces. It is typically determined using a pycnometer, based on Archimedes' principle, by measuring the volume of water displaced by a known mass of soil.

Materials Required

Oven-dried soil sample, 100 ml graduated measuring cylinder (or pycnometer), Soil core sampler (for bulk density), Balance (accurate to 0.01 g), Oven (105°C), Spatula, Distilled water, Desiccator.

Part A: Bulk Density (Core Method)

Formula

$$\text{Bulk Density (g/cm}^3\text{)} = \frac{\text{Mass of oven-dry soil (g)}}{\text{Volume of soil (cm}^3\text{)}}$$

Procedure

1. **Sample Collection:**
   - Collect an undisturbed soil sample using a core sampler of known volume (e.g., 100 cm³).
2. **Drying:**
   - Weigh the moist soil sample.
   - Place the soil in an oven at 105°C for 24 hours to remove moisture.
3. **Weighing:**
   - Cool the soil in a desiccator, then weigh the dry soil.
4. **Calculation:**
   - Measure or note the volume of the core sampler.
   - Use the formula to calculate bulk density.

Observation Table:

Parameter	Value
Weight of empty core (g)	
Weight of core + moist soil (g)	
Weight of oven-dry soil (g)	
Volume of core (cm^3)	
Bulk Density (g/cm^3)	

Part B: Particle Density

Formula

$$\text{Particle Density } (g/cm^3) = \frac{\text{Mass of oven-dry soil (g)}}{\text{Volume of soil solids } (cm^3)}$$

Procedure (Using Pycnometer or Flask Method)

1. **Weighing:**
   - Weigh about 10 g of oven-dry soil.
2. **Filling Pycnometer:**
   - Transfer the soil into a 100 ml pycnometer or measuring flask.
   - Fill the flask with distilled water to the 100 ml mark.
   - Ensure no air bubbles remain (use gentle tapping or vacuum if needed).
3. **Weighing:**
   - Weigh the pycnometer with soil and water.
   - Also weigh a pycnometer filled with only water to the same mark.
4. **Calculation:**
   - Use the difference in water displacement to find the volume of soil solids.

Observation Table

Parameter	**Value**
Weight of oven-dry soil used (g)	
Volume of water displaced (cm^3)	
Particle Density (g/cm^3)	

Typical Values

- **Bulk Density**:
    - Sandy soils: 1.4–1.7 g/cm^3
    - Loamy soils: 1.2–1.6 g/cm^3
    - Clay soils: 1.0–1.4 g/cm^3
- **Particle Density**:
    - Usually ranges between 2.60–2.75 g/cm^3 (depends on mineral content)

Conclusion

- A high bulk density indicates compacted soil, which can restrict root growth and water movement.
- Particle density reflects the type of minerals present in the soil.
- The difference between particle and bulk density helps estimate porosity.

Precautions:

- Ensure complete drying of soil before weighing.
- Avoid air bubbles during water displacement.
- Calibrate volume measurements accurately.

Experiment 04

Porosity and Infiltration Rate of Soil

Principle

Soil porosity refers to the fraction of the total soil volume that is occupied by pore spaces, which can be filled with air or water. It is a critical property influencing water retention, movement, and availability to plants.

Infiltration rate is the speed at which water enters the soil surface, affecting groundwater recharge and surface runoff. These properties are influenced by soil texture, structure, compaction, and organic matter content. Understanding porosity and infiltration rates is essential for effective soil and water management practices.

Materials Required

Oven-dried soil samples, Graduated cylinder (100 mL), Weighing balance, Beakers (250 mL), Double-ring infiltrometer (inner ring: 30 cm diameter; outer ring: 60 cm diameter), Stopwatch, Measuring scale or ruler, Distilled water, Plastic sheet or tarp, Hammer or mallet, Notebook and pen for observations .

Procedure

A. Determination of Soil Porosity

- Collect a representative soil sample and air-dry it. Remove any debris or organic matter.
- Fill a graduated cylinder with a known volume (V) of dry soil. Record this volume.
- Slowly add distilled water to the cylinder until the water reaches the top of the soil without overflowing. Record the volume of water added (V_w).
- Calculation: Porosity (%) = (V_w / V) × 100

Typical Porosity Ranges

Soil Type	Porosity (%)
Sandy Soil	30–35%
Loamy Soil	40–50%
Clay Soil	50–60%

B. Determination of Infiltration Rate Using Double-Ring Infiltrometer

- Choose a flat, undisturbed area for the test. Remove any surface debris.

- Place the double-ring infiltrometer on the soil surface. Use a hammer or mallet to drive both rings vertically into the soil to a depth of 15 cm, ensuring they are concentric and level.
- Place a plastic sheet inside the inner ring to prevent soil disturbance during water addition.
- Fill both rings with water to a depth of 10 cm. Remove the plastic sheet carefully to start the test.
- Start the stopwatch immediately after removing the sheet. Record the drop in water level in the inner ring at regular intervals (e.g., every 5 minutes) for a total duration of 60 minutes or until a steady infiltration rate is observed.
- Calculation: Infiltration Rate (cm/hr) = (Initial water depth - Final water depth) / Time elapsed (in hours)

Precautions

- Ensure the soil surface is level and free from cracks or vegetation.
- Avoid disturbing the soil structure during ring installation.
- Maintain equal water levels in both rings to prevent lateral flow.
- Conduct the test under calm weather conditions to minimize evaporation.
- Repeat the test at multiple locations for accurate representation.

Experiment 05

Soil Moisture Content Determination (Gravimetric and Tensiometer Methods)

Principle

Soil moisture content is a critical parameter influencing plant growth, soil microbial activity, and various soil physical properties. Accurate determination of soil moisture aids in effective irrigation management, crop yield optimization, and understanding soil-water-plant relationships.

Gravimetric Method involves measuring the weight loss of a soil sample upon drying, which corresponds to the water content. It provides a direct and accurate measurement of soil moisture on a dry weight basis.

Tensiometer Method or *Tensiometers* measure the soil water tension (matric potential), indicating how tightly water is held in the soil. This method is useful for in-situ monitoring of soil moisture status, especially in the root zone.

Materials Required

For Gravimetric Method:

Soil samples. Moisture tins or aluminium containers, Analytical balance (precision of 0.01 g), Drying oven (maintained at 105°C), Desiccator, Tongs or heat-resistant gloves.

For Tensiometer Method:

Tensiometer (appropriate length for the desired soil depth), Auger or soil core, Water (preferably de-aerated), Vacuum pump or syringe (for removing air bubbles), Sealant (e.g., clay or silicone), Notebook and pen for recording readings.

Procedure

A. Gravimetric Method

1. **Sample Collection:**
   - Collect soil samples from the desired depth using a soil auger or corer.
   - Place the samples in moisture tins and seal immediately to prevent moisture loss.
2. **Weighing Wet Soil:**

   Weigh the moisture tin with the wet soil sample using the analytical balance. Record the weight (W_{wet}).
3. **Drying:**

Place the moisture tins in the drying oven at 105°C for 24 hours or until a constant weight is achieved.

4. **Cooling**:

   After drying, transfer the tins to a desiccator to cool to room temperature, preventing moisture absorption from the air.

5. **Weighing Dry Soil**:

   Weigh the moisture tin with the dry soil sample. Record the weight (W_{dry}).

6. **Calculation**:

   Determine the moisture content using the formula:
   Moisture Content (%) = ((W_{wet} - W_{dry}) / W_{dry}) × 100

B. Tensiometer Method

1. **Preparation of Tensiometer**:
   - Fill the tensiometer with de-aerated water, ensuring no air bubbles are present.
   - Place the tensiometer in a vertical position and allow it to equilibrate.

2. **Installation**:
   - Use an auger to create a hole in the soil to the desired depth.
   - Insert the tensiometer into the hole, ensuring the ceramic tip is in good contact with the soil.
   - Seal the area around the tensiometer to prevent air entry.

3. **Reading Measurements**:
   - Allow the tensiometer to equilibrate with the soil moisture (this may take several hours).
   - Read the tension value from the gauge, which indicates the soil water tension in centibars or kilopascals.

4. **Maintenance**:
   - Regularly check the water level in the tensiometer and refill as necessary.

- Ensure the device remains free of air bubbles for accurate readings.

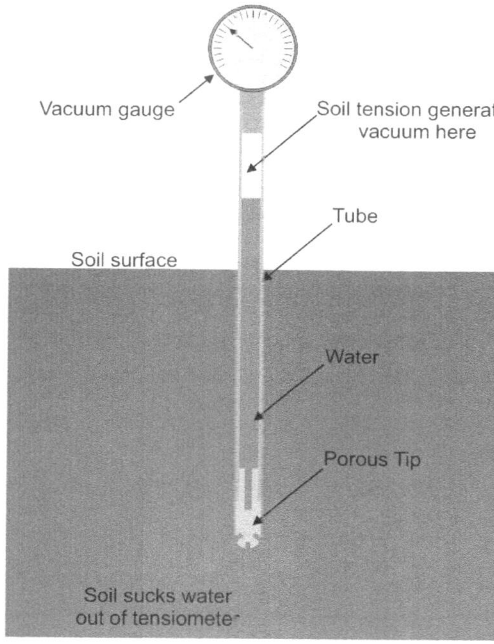

Typical Soil Moisture Ranges from Tensiometer Readings

Soil Tension (centibars)	Soil Moisture Condition
0 – 10	Saturated
10 – 30	Field capacity
30 – 60	Good moisture for crops
60 – 80	Begin irrigation
> 80	Dry soil, stressed crops

Precautions

- Ensure moisture tins are sealed immediately after sample collection to prevent moisture loss.
- Avoid contamination of samples during handling.
- Do not open the oven frequently during drying to maintain a consistent temperature.

Experiment 06

Determination of Water Holding Capacity (WHC) of Soil

Principle

Water Holding Capacity (WHC) refers to the maximum amount of water that a soil can retain against gravity after being saturated and allowed to drain. It is a critical parameter indicating the soil's ability to supply water to plants between irrigation or rainfall events.

Materials Required

Air-dried, sieved soil sample, Weighing balance (precision of 0.01 g), Perforated soil box or container, Filter paper, Beaker or tray, Water, Drying oven capable of maintaining 105 ± 5°C, Desiccator.

Procedure

1. **Preparation :**
   - Place a filter paper inside the perforated bottom of the soil box. Weigh the empty box and record its weight as W_0.
2. **Filling Soil :**
   - Fill the box with a known weight of air-dried soil and record the combined weight as W_1.
3. **Saturation :**
   - Place the soil-filled box in a tray containing water. Allow it to saturate for 12 hours to ensure complete water absorption.
4. **Drainage :**
   - Remove the box, wipe the exterior to remove excess water, and allow it to drain until water ceases to drip. Weigh the saturated soil box and record the weight as W_2.
5. **Drying :**
   - Remove the soil from the box, place it in a drying oven at 105 ± 5°C for 24 hours to remove all moisture.
6. **Final Weighing :**
   - After drying, cool the soil in a desiccator to room temperature and weigh to obtain the dry weight, recorded as W_3.

Calculation

The Water Holding Capacity (WHC) is calculated using the following formula:

$$\text{WHC}(\%) = \frac{W_2 - W_3}{W_3 - W_0} \times 100$$

Where:

W_0: Weight of the empty soil box (g)

W_2: Weight of the soil box with saturated soil after drainage (g)

W_3: Weight of the oven-dried soil after saturation (g)

This formula calculates the percentage of water retained by the soil after saturation and drainage, relative to the dry weight of the soil.

Precautions

- Ensure uniform saturation of the soil without overflooding.
- Avoid loss of soil particles during drainage.
- Use consistent sample sizes for comparative analysis.
- Ensure the oven maintains a consistent temperature of 105 ± 5°C.
- Use a desiccator to cool samples before weighing to prevent moisture absorption from the air.

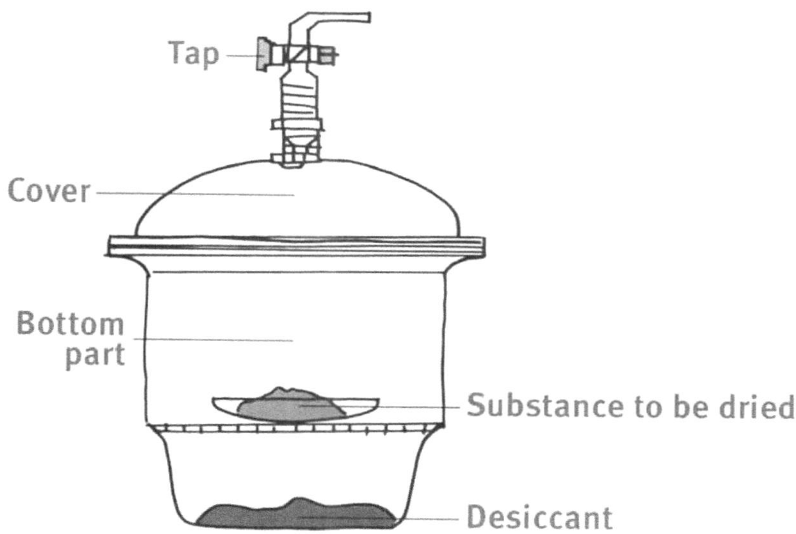

Diagrammatic view of a desiccator

Module 2

Soil Chemistry

Experiment 07

Soil pH and Electrical Conductivity (EC) Determination

Principles

Soil pH is a measure of the hydrogen ion activity in the soil solution. It is an important indicator of soil chemical properties, influencing nutrient availability, microbial activity, and plant growth. It is measured using a pH meter in a soil-water suspension, typically in a 1:2.5 soil-to-water ratio.

Electrical conductivity (EC) reflects the soil's ability to conduct an electrical current, which is directly related to the concentration of soluble salts in the soil. It provides an index of soil salinity. EC is measured using a conductivity meter, typically in a 1:2.5 or saturated paste extract.

Materials Required

Soil sample (air-dried and sieved), Distilled water, pH meter (glass electrode type), EC meter (conductivity bridge), Beakers (100 mL and 250 mL), Measuring cylinder (50 mL), Glass rod (for stirring), Filter paper (Whatman No. 42 or equivalent), Wash bottle, Digital balance (precision: 0.01 g).

Procedure

A. Determination of Soil pH

- Take 10 g of air-dried, sieved soil in a 100 mL beaker.
- Add 25 mL of distilled water (soil:water ratio of 1:2.5).
- Stir the suspension well using a glass rod and allow it to stand for 30 minutes, stirring intermittently.
- Calibrate the pH meter with standard buffer solutions (pH 4.0, 7.0, and 9.2).
- Immerse the pH electrode into the supernatant and record the pH value once stabilized.
- Rinse the electrode with distilled water after each reading.

Observation Table (pH)

Sample No.	Soil:Water Ratio	pH Value
...	1:2.5	...

Interpretation of pH Values

pH Range	Soil Reaction
< 4.5	Extremely acidic
4.5 – 5.5	Strongly acidic
5.6 – 6.5	Moderately acidic
6.6 – 7.3	Neutral
7.4 – 8.4	Moderately alkaline
> 8.5	Strongly alkaline

B. Determination of Electrical Conductivity (EC)

- Take another 10 g of the soil sample in a clean beaker.
- Add 25 mL of distilled water (1:2.5 ratio).
- Stir and let it stand for 30 minutes, stirring occasionally.
- Calibrate the EC meter with a standard KCl solution.
- Insert the EC electrode into the supernatant and note the EC reading in dS/m.
- Rinse the electrode thoroughly between samples.

Interpretation of EC Values

EC (dS/m)	Salinity Class	Suitability for Crops
< 1.0	Normal	Suitable for most crops
1.0 – 2.0	Slightly saline	May affect salt-sensitive crops
2.0 – 4.0	Moderately saline	Restricts growth of sensitive crops
> 4.0	Strongly saline	Only tolerant crops survive

Precautions

- Use distilled water only, as tap water may alter the pH and EC values.
- Ensure proper calibration of both pH and EC meters before use.
- Avoid contamination of samples or electrodes.
- Stir the soil-water suspension gently to prevent damage to the electrodes.
- Maintain consistent soil-to-water ratios for accuracy and comparability.
- Clean and store electrodes as per the manufacturer's instructions.

Experiment 08

Estimation of Organic Carbon in Soil (Walkley-Black Method)

Principle

The *Walkley-Black method* is a widely used wet oxidation procedure for estimating organic carbon in soil. Organic carbon in the soil is oxidized by an excess of potassium dichromate ($K_2Cr_2O_7$) in the presence of concentrated sulfuric acid (H_2SO_4), which generates heat and facilitates oxidation. The unreacted $K_2Cr_2O_7$ is then titrated with ferrous ammonium sulfate (FAS) using diphenylamine as an internal indicator. The amount of dichromate consumed is directly proportional to the oxidizable organic carbon. Since this method does not oxidize 100% of organic carbon, a correction factor (typically 1.33) is applied.

Reaction

$$K_2Cr_2O_7 + H_2SO_4 + C_{organic} \rightarrow Cr_3^{+} + CO_2 + H_2O$$

Materials and Reagents Required

Soil sample (air-dried and sieved), 1 N potassium dichromate ($K_2Cr_2O_7$) solution, Concentrated sulfuric acid (H_2SO_4), 0.5 N ferrous ammonium sulfate (FAS) solution, Diphenylamine indicator (1% in sulfuric acid), Distilled water, Burettes, pipettes, and conical flasks, Measuring cylinders, Analytical balance, Glass funnel, Beakers.

Procedure

- Weigh 1.0 g of finely ground, air-dried soil into a 500 mL conical flask.
- Add 10 mL of 1 N $K_2Cr_2O_7$ solution using a pipette.
- Add 20 mL of concentrated H_2SO_4 directly to the flask (handle carefully).
- Swirl the flask gently for 1 minute to mix thoroughly.
- Let the mixture stand for 30 minutes for complete oxidation.
- After cooling, add 200 mL of distilled water to dilute the contents.
- Add 10 drops of diphenylamine indicator (solution turns violet-blue).
- Titrate the excess dichromate with 0.5 N FAS until the color changes from blue to green, then to brilliant green endpoint.
- Run a blank simultaneously (without soil) following the same steps.
- Calculate the amount of organic carbon using the titration values and apply a correction factor.

Calculations

Let:

- B = Volume (mL) of FAS used for blank
- S = Volume (mL) of FAS used for sample

- N = Normality of FAS

$$\text{Organic Carbon (\%)} = \frac{(B-S) \times N \times 0.003 \times 1.33 \times 100}{\text{Weight of soil (g)}}$$

Interpretation

Organic Carbon (%)	Organic Matter Status
< 0.5	Low
0.5 – 0.75	Medium
> 0.75	High

Precautions

- Use concentrated sulfuric acid carefully—always wear protective gear.
- Ensure complete mixing during acid addition to avoid localized heating.
- Avoid exposure to fumes; work in a fume hood if possible.
- The endpoint should be identified accurately; practice with indicator helps.
- All glassware must be clean and dry before use.
- The correction factor (1.33) should be applied unless recovery efficiency is known.

Experiment 09

Estimation of Available Nitrogen in Soil (Alkaline $KMnO_4$ Method)

Principle

The *alkaline $KMnO_4$ method* is based on the principle that a portion of organic nitrogen in soil is readily oxidizable under alkaline conditions. In this method, $KMnO_4$ acts as an oxidizing agent in the presence of NaOH, liberating ammonia (NH_3) from easily oxidizable organic nitrogen compounds. The released NH_3 is distilled and absorbed in boric acid, and then titrated with standard sulfuric acid (H_2SO_4). The amount of acid required is proportional to the amount of available nitrogen in the soil.

Materials and Reagents Required

Soil sample (air-dried, sieved through 2 mm sieve), 0.32% potassium permanganate ($KMnO_4$) solution, 2.5% sodium hydroxide (NaOH) solution, 2% boric acid (H_3BO_3) solution with mixed indicator (bromocresol green and methyl red), Standard 0.01 N sulfuric acid (H_2SO_4), Kjeldahl distillation unit, Conical flasks, Measuring cylinders and pipettes, Burette, Beakers, Distilled water, Glass funnel, Analytical balance.

Procedure

- Weigh 20 g of soil and place in the distillation flask.
- Add 100 mL of distilled water to the flask.
- Add 100 mL of 0.32% $KMnO_4$ and 100 mL of 2.5% NaOH solutions.
- Immediately connect the flask to the Kjeldahl distillation unit.
- Place a conical flask containing 25 mL of 2% boric acid and a few drops of mixed indicator at the outlet to collect the distilled NH_3.
- Distill until about 50 mL of distillate is collected (usually in 30 minutes).
- Titrate the distillate with 0.01 N H_2SO_4 until the color changes from green to pink.
- Run a blank without soil using the same reagents.
- Calculate available nitrogen using the titration values.

Calculations

Let:

- T = Volume of H_2SO_4 used for sample (mL)
- B = Volume of H_2SO_4 used for blank (mL)
- N = Normality of H_2SO_4

$$\text{Available N (mg/kg)} = \frac{(T - B) \times N \times 14}{\text{Weight of soil (g)}} \times 1000$$

For 20 g soil and 0.01 N H_2SO_4:

$$\text{Available N (kg/ha)} = (T - B) \times 14 \times 2.24$$

Interpretation

Available N (kg/ha)	**Rating**
< 280	Low
280 – 560	Medium
> 560	High

(To convert ppm to kg/ha, multiply by **2.24** for 15 cm soil depth with bulk density of 1.3 g/cm^3)

Precautions

- All glassware must be clean and free of NH_3 traces.
- Distill slowly to prevent bumping and loss of ammonia.
- Ensure the joint connections in the distillation unit are airtight.
- Always use freshly prepared $KMnO_4$ and NaOH solutions.
- Properly standardize the sulfuric acid solution before titration.
- The endpoint must be observed accurately using the mixed indicator.

Experiment 10

Estimation of Available Phosphorus in Soil (Olsen's Method)

Principle

The *Olsen's method* is commonly used for estimating available phosphorus in neutral to alkaline soils (pH > 6.5). It involves extraction of phosphorus using 0.5 M sodium bicarbonate ($NaHCO_3$) at pH 8.5, which replaces adsorbed phosphate ions from soil colloids into solution. The extracted phosphorus reacts with ammonium molybdate and antimony potassium tartrate in an acidic medium to form a phosphor molybdenum blue complex, which is then reduced by ascorbic acid. The intensity of the blue color is measured using a spectrophotometer at 880 nm, and the phosphorus content is determined from a standard curve.

Materials and Reagents Required

Soil sample (air-dried, sieved), 0.5 M sodium bicarbonate ($NaHCO_3$), pH adjusted to 8.5, Activated charcoal (analytical grade), Ammonium molybdate solution, Antimony potassium tartrate solution, Ascorbic acid (freshly prepared), Sulfuric acid (H_2SO_4), Standard phosphorus solution (KH_2PO_4), Whatman No. 42 filter paper, Colorimeter or spectrophotometer (set at 880 nm), Volumetric flasks, beakers, pipettes, and conical flasks, Shaker or mechanical agitator.

Procedure

- Weigh 2.5 g of air-dried soil into a 100 mL conical flask.
- Add 50 mL of 0.5 M $NaHCO_3$ solution.
- Add a pinch (about 0.5 g) of activated charcoal to decolorize organic matter.
- Shake the mixture on a mechanical shaker for 30 minutes.
- Filter the contents through Whatman No. 42 filter paper.
- Pipette 5 mL of the clear filtrate into a 25 mL volumetric flask.
- Add:
    - 5 mL of ammonium molybdate solution
    - 1 mL of antimony potassium tartrate solution
    - 5 mL of 1 M sulfuric acid
    - 3 mL of ascorbic acid solution (add this last)
- Make up the volume to 25 mL with distilled water and mix well.
- Allow the color to develop for 30 minutes.
- Measure the absorbance at 880 nm using a spectrophotometer.
- Determine the phosphorus content using a standard curve prepared with known concentrations of KH_2PO_4.

Calculations

Determine available phosphorus (mg/kg or kg/ha) using the absorbance value and standard curve.

$$\text{Available P (mg/kg)} = \frac{C \times V}{W}$$

Where:

- C = Concentration from the standard curve (mg/L)
- V = Volume of extractant (L)
- W = Weight of soil (kg)

To convert to kg/ha, multiply by **2.24**.

Interpretation

Available Phosphorus (kg/ha)	**Rating**
< 10	Low
10 – 25	Medium
> 25	High

Precautions

- Use freshly prepared reagents, especially ascorbic acid.
- Maintain pH of $NaHCO_3$ at 8.5 for accurate extraction.
- Use activated charcoal only in appropriate quantity to avoid phosphate adsorption.
- Avoid contamination of glassware and ensure proper rinsing.
- Use a blank for spectrophotometric calibration.
- Calibrate the colorimeter or spectrophotometer before use.

Experiment 11

Determination of Available Potassium in Soil (Flame Photometric Method)

Principle

Available potassium in soil includes exchangeable and water-soluble forms, which are readily accessible to plants. These forms are extracted using 1N ammonium acetate (NH_4OAc) at neutral pH (7.0), which replaces exchangeable potassium ions (K^+) held on soil colloids by ammonium ions. The potassium in the filtrate is then quantified using a flame photometer, where the intensity of light emitted at 766.5 nm is directly proportional to the potassium concentration in the sample.

Materials Required

Air-dried, sieved soil sample, 1N ammonium acetate solution (NH_4OAc), pH 7.0, Potassium standard solutions (prepared from KCl), Flame photometer (calibrated at 766.5 nm), Shaker or mechanical agitator, Whatman No. 42 filter paper, Conical flasks (100 mL), Volumetric flasks, pipettes, beakers, Distilled water, Glass funnels.

Procedure

- Weigh 5 g of air-dried, sieved soil into a 100 mL conical flask.
- Add 25 mL of 1N NH_4OAc (pH 7.0) solution.
- Shake the flask on a mechanical shaker for 30 minutes.
- Filter the extract through Whatman No. 42 filter paper.
- Collect the clear filtrate in a clean container.
- Prepare a standard curve using KCl solutions of known potassium concentrations (e.g., 0, 2, 4, 6, 8, 10 ppm).
- Calibrate the flame photometer with the standards.
- Aspirate the soil extract into the flame photometer and record the reading.
- Determine the potassium concentration of the sample using the standard curve.

Calculations

$$\text{Available K (kg/ha)} = C \times V \times f$$

Where:

- C = Concentration of potassium in extract (ppm or mg/L)
- V = Volume of extractant used (L)
- f = Conversion factor (for 5 g soil and 25 mL extractant, f = 8.96)

Or directly:

Available K (kg/ha) = ppm K $\times$ 11.2

Interpretation

Available Potassium (ppm)	Rating
< 60	Low
60 – 150	Medium
> 150	High

Precautions

- Ensure flame photometer calibration with freshly prepared standard K solutions.
- Use deionized or distilled water for preparing reagents.
- Avoid contamination by rinsing all glassware with ammonium acetate before use.
- Handle flame photometer carefully and regularly check for consistent flame and air pressure.
- Ensure the pH of NH_4OAc is adjusted accurately to 7.0.
- Do not reuse filter paper or pipettes without cleaning to avoid cross-contamination.

Experiment 12

Measurement of Cation Exchange Capacity (CEC) of Soil

Principle

Cation Exchange Capacity (CEC) refers to the total capacity of soil to hold exchangeable cations. It is an essential soil property influencing soil fertility, nutrient retention, and buffering capacity. CEC is commonly measured by saturating soil with a specific cation (commonly ammonium), displacing it with another (usually sodium or potassium), and determining the amount of exchanged cation using titration or instrumental methods.

Materials and Reagents

Soil sample (air-dried, sieved through 2 mm sieve), Ammonium acetate solution (1 N, pH 7.0), Ethanol (95%), Potassium chloride (KCl) solution (1 N) or sodium chloride (NaCl), for displacement, Distilled water, Beakers, funnels, conical flasks, Whatman No. 42 filter paper, Mechanical shaker, Measuring cylinders and pipettes, Titration setup or flame photometer for measurement.

Procedure

1. **Saturation with Ammonium:**
   - Weigh 10 g of soil into a 250 ml conical flask.
   - Add 100 ml of 1 N ammonium acetate solution (pH 7.0).
   - Shake for 30 minutes on a mechanical shaker.
   - Filter the mixture using Whatman No. 42 filter paper.
   - Repeat the extraction twice and discard the filtrates.
2. **Removal of Excess Ammonium Acetate:**
   - Wash the soil residue on the filter paper with 95% ethanol (3 × 25 ml) to remove excess ammonium acetate.
3. **Displacement of Adsorbed Ammonium:**
   - Leach the soil with 100 ml of 1 N KCl or NaCl solution.
   - Collect the leachate in a clean flask.
4. **Determination of Ammonium:**
   - Determine the amount of ammonium in the leachate by distillation followed by titration or use a spectrophotometer or Kjeldahl apparatus.
5. **Calculation:**

$$\text{CEC (meq/100g soil)} = \frac{\text{mg of NH4 + extracted} \times 100}{14 \times \text{weight of soil in g}}$$

Observation Table (Sample)

Parameter	Value
Weight of soil (g)	10
Volume of KCl used (ml)	100
NH_4^+ in filtrate (mg)	50
CEC (meq/100g soil)	Calculated

Interpretation

CEC (meq/100g)	Soil Fertility Indicator
< 5	Very Low
5 – 15	Low
15 – 25	Medium
> 25	High

Precautions

- Use properly sieved and air-dried soil samples.
- Ensure complete saturation and proper washing steps.
- Avoid contamination during displacement and filtration.
- Use standardised reagents for accurate results.

Experiment 13

Soil Fertility Evaluation and Nutrient Deficiency Diagnosis

Principle

Soil fertility refers to the soil's ability to supply essential nutrients to plants in adequate amounts and proper proportions. Evaluation of soil fertility involves both chemical analysis of soils and observation of crop response to nutrient availability. Nutrient deficiency diagnosis can be conducted through:

- Soil testing for available macro- and micronutrients,
- Visual symptoms on plants (chlorosis, necrosis, stunting, etc.),
- Plant tissue analysis, and
- Field trials or biological assays (e.g., pot culture tests).

Each nutrient deficiency presents characteristic symptoms in plants and is correlated with insufficient levels in the soil or plant tissues. A comprehensive diagnosis combines lab-based soil test values with field-based observations.

Materials Required

Soil sample (air-dried and sieved), Field sampling tools (auger, trowel, sample bags), Plant samples (for tissue analysis), Fertilizer response data or crop growth records, Standard deficiency symptom charts (e.g., for N, P, K, Fe, Zn, etc.), Pot or field setup for bioassay (optional), Reagents and equipment required for; pH (pH meter); EC (EC meter); Organic carbon (Walkley–Black method); Available N (alkaline $KMnO_4$ method); Available P (Olsen's or Bray's method); Available K (NH_4OAc extraction and flame photometry); Micronutrients (DTPA extraction and AAS).

Procedure

1. **Soil Sampling**

- Collect representative soil samples from the top 15–20 cm using a clean auger.
- Mix multiple cores to form a composite sample.
- Air-dry, grind, and sieve through a 2 mm mesh.

2. **Soil Analysis**

- Determine pH, EC, organic carbon, and available N, P, K, and micronutrients using standard soil testing protocols (refer to previous experiments).

3. **Nutrient Interpretation**

- Compare soil test values with critical levels for specific crops.
- Categorize nutrient levels as low, medium, or high.

4. **Plant Symptom Observation**

- Observe plant leaves, stems, and growth for visual deficiency symptoms (e.g., yellowing, purpling, stunting).
- Refer to standardized nutrient deficiency charts.

5. **Tissue Analysis (optional)**

- Collect recently matured leaves.
- Analyze for nutrient concentrations in tissue.

6. **Crop Response Trials (optional)**

- Set up a pot or field trial with and without added nutrients.
- Observe plant growth response to identify limiting nutrients.

Interpretation

- Nutrients below critical range indicate deficiency and need for fertilisation.
- Soil pH outside optimal range may affect nutrient availability.
- Soil texture and organic matter influence fertility and nutrient holding capacity.
- Plant symptoms support diagnosis of nutrient limitations.

Precautions

- Use clean tools to avoid contamination during sampling.
- Collect soil samples when the field is not waterlogged or overly dry.
- Store soil samples in labeled, clean, and dry containers.
- Maintain consistency in sampling depth and methodology.
- Interpret results with reference to crop-specific critical limits.
- Confirm diagnosis using multiple approaches (soil + symptoms + plant analysis).

Module 3

Soil Microbiology & Biology

Experiment 14

Microbial Biomass Carbon Estimation

Principle

Soil *microbial biomass carbon* (MBC) refers to the living component of soil organic matter, excluding plant roots and fauna larger than 5–10 μm. The chloroform fumigation-extraction method is commonly used to estimate MBC. In this method, microbial cells are lysed by exposure to chloroform vapours, and the released organic C is extracted using a salt solution (commonly 0.5 M K_2SO_4). The extractable C in fumigated and non-fumigated samples is determined, and the difference is used to calculate microbial biomass carbon using a conversion factor.

Materials and Reagents/Equipment Required

Fresh soil sample (field-moist), Chloroform (ethanol-free), Desiccator with vacuum pump, Whatman No. 42 filter paper, 0.5 M Potassium sulphate (K_2SO_4), 100 mL conical flasks, Shaker (horizontal), Spectrophotometer (or TOC analyser, if available), Glassware: pipettes, measuring cylinders, beakers, Burette, retort stand, Distilled water, Fume hood (for safe handling of chloroform), Incubator (optional for drying), Aluminium foil/parafilm, Labels and marker.

Procedure

1. Sample Preparation

- Collect fresh, field-moist soil and pass it through a 2 mm sieve.
- Weigh two sets of 10 g soil samples into conical flasks — one set for fumigated and one for non-fumigated.

2. Fumigation

- Place the fumigated set into a desiccator along with a beaker of ethanol-free chloroform.
- Evacuate the desiccator using a vacuum pump to vaporise the chloroform.
- Allow fumigation to proceed for 24 hours in dark conditions.
- After fumigation, remove the chloroform and aerate the samples for 30 minutes under a fume hood.

3. Extraction

- Add 40 mL of 0.5 M K_2SO_4 to each soil sample (fumigated and non-fumigated).
- Shake the samples horizontally for 30 minutes.
- Filter through Whatman No. 42 filter paper.

4. Estimation

- Measure the organic carbon content in the extract using a spectrophotometric method (e.g., potassium dichromate oxidation) or a TOC analyser.

5. Calculation

Microbial Biomass Carbon (MBC) is calculated as:

$$MBC = \frac{E_{Cf} - EC_{nf}}{k_{EC}}$$

Where:

- EC_x = Extractable organic C (mg C/kg soil) from fumigated (f) and non-fumigated (nf) samples
- k_{EC} = 0.38 (conversion factor)

Observation Table (Sample)

Sample ID	Treatment	Extractable C (mg/kg)	MBC (mg/kg)
S1	Fumigated (E_{Cf})	280	
S1	Non-fumigated (EC_{nf})	190	

$$MBC = \frac{280-190}{0.38} = 236.84 \text{ mg/kg}$$

Precautions

- Always handle chloroform inside a fume hood; it is highly toxic and volatile.
- Ensure complete vapourisation of chloroform in the desiccator.
- Use ethanol-free chloroform only.
- Prevent microbial activity post-extraction by filtering immediately.
- Avoid contamination of soil samples.
- Maintain consistency in sample weights and shaking times.

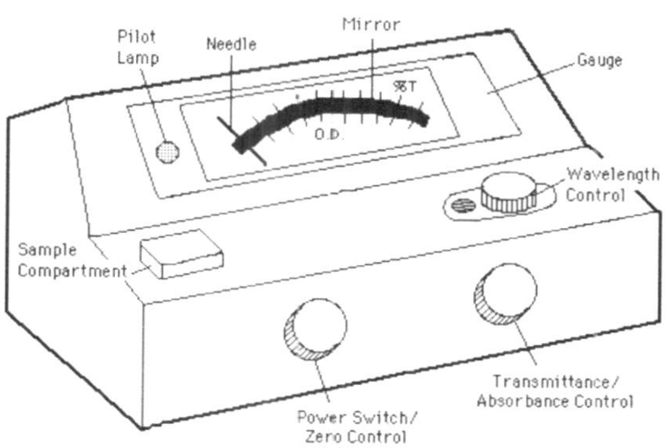

A Spectrophotometer

Experiment 15

Enumeration of Soil Microorganisms (Fungi, Bacteria, Actinomycetes by Serial Dilution)

Principle

Soil contains a diverse range of microorganisms such as bacteria, fungi, and actinomycetes. The *serial dilution and plate count technique* is a widely used method to estimate their population. A soil suspension is serially diluted, and aliquots are plated on specific selective media. After incubation, the colonies are counted and expressed as colony-forming units (CFU) per gram of soil.

Materials and Reagents/Equipment Required

Fresh soil sample, Sterile distilled water, Conical flasks and test tubes, Serial dilution tubes (typically 10^{-1} to 10^{-6}), Sterile pipettes (1 mL and 10 mL), Petri plates, Inoculation loop, Laminar airflow chamber or sterile environment, Autoclave, Incubator (set at 28–30°C), Marker and labels

Specific media

- Nutrient agar (for bacteria)
- Potato dextrose agar (PDA) (for fungi)
- Actinomycetes isolation agar (for actinomycetes)

Procedure

1. **Sample Preparation:**
   - Weigh 10 g of fresh soil into a 250 mL conical flask.
   - Add 90 mL of sterile distilled water to make a 1:10 suspension (10^{-1} dilution).
   - Shake vigorously on a shaker for 15–30 minutes.
2. **Serial Dilution:**
   - Prepare dilution tubes with 9 mL of sterile distilled water.
   - Transfer 1 mL from the soil suspension into the first tube to get 10^{-2} dilution.
   - Continue serial dilutions up to 10^{-6}, as needed.
3. **Plating:**
   - Using a sterile pipette, take 0.1 mL from each appropriate dilution and plate it on:
     - Nutrient agar for bacteria
     - PDA for fungi
     - Actinomycetes isolation agar for actinomycetes
   - Spread the inoculum evenly using a sterile spreader.

4. **Incubation:**
   - Incubate the plates:
     - Bacteria: 24–48 hours at 28–30°C
     - Fungi: 3–5 days at 25–28°C
     - Actinomycetes: 5–7 days at 28°C

5. **Counting and Recording:**
   - After incubation, count colonies using a colony counter.
   - Multiply by the dilution factor to obtain CFU/g of soil.

Observation Table (Sample)

Microorganism	Dilution	No. of Colonies	CFU/g Soil
Bacteria	10^{-5}	65	6.5×10^{6}
Fungi	10^{-3}	22	2.2×10^{4}
Actinomycetes	10^{-4}	35	3.5×10^{5}

Precautions

- Maintain strict sterility during the process to avoid contamination.
- Prepare and autoclave media properly before use.
- Use separate pipettes and spreaders for each dilution and microorganism.
- Label all plates clearly to avoid confusion.
- Avoid over-incubation which may lead to colony merging.

Experiment 16

Soil Respiration Measurement

Principle

Soil respiration is a key indicator of microbial activity and soil health. It refers to the release of carbon dioxide (CO_2) from soil as a result of microbial decomposition of organic matter and root respiration. Measuring soil respiration provides insight into biological activity and organic matter turnover. The commonly used method involves capturing CO_2 evolved from soil in a sodium hydroxide (NaOH) solution and quantifying it by back-titration with standard acid.

Materials and Reagents/Equipment Required

Fresh soil sample (moist), Airtight incubation jars or containers, Small beakers or vials (to hold NaOH solution), 0.5 N Sodium hydroxide (NaOH) solution, Barium chloride ($BaCl_2$) or barium hydroxide ($Ba(OH)_2$) (optional, for CO_2 precipitation), 0.5 N Hydrochloric acid (HCl) or sulfuric acid (H_2SO_4) for titration, Phenolphthalein indicator, Burette, pipettes, and conical flasks, Analytical balance, Incubator or a constant room temperature.

Procedure

1. **Sample Preparation:**
   - Weigh 50 g of moist soil into an airtight glass jar or incubation container.
2. **CO_2 Trapping Setup:**
   - Place a small open beaker or vial containing 10 mL of 0.5 N NaOH inside the jar (without touching the soil).
   - Seal the container airtight to prevent atmospheric CO_2 contamination.
3. **Incubation:**
   - Incubate the jar at 25–30°C for 24 to 72 hours depending on the experiment duration.
4. **Termination:**
   - After incubation, remove the NaOH solution carefully.
5. **Titration:**
   - Add 2–3 drops of phenolphthalein indicator to the NaOH solution.
   - Titrate with 0.5 N HCl until the pink colour disappears (endpoint).
   - Run a blank using NaOH kept in a sealed container without soil to correct for atmospheric CO_2.
6. **Calculation:**

- The difference in acid used for blank and sample represents the amount of CO_2 evolved.

Observation Table (Sample)

Sample ID	Volume of HCl for Blank (mL)	Volume of HCl for Sample (mL)	Volume Difference (mL)	CO_2 Evolved (mg CO_2/50g soil)
A	9.8	6.2	3.6	79.2

CO_2 evolved = Volume difference × Normality × 22 (mg CO_2 per mL of 1N HCl)

Precautions

- Use airtight containers to avoid CO_2 loss.
- Avoid contamination of NaOH by external CO_2.
- Ensure consistent temperature during incubation.
- Perform blank titration for accurate correction.
- Use freshly prepared and standardised solutions.

Experiment 17

Vermicomposting and Its Effects on Soil Nutrient Status

Principle

Vermicomposting is the biological decomposition of organic waste using earthworms, producing nutrient-rich compost. Earthworms enhance microbial activity and mineralisation, improving soil nutrient status. By comparing pre- and post-vermicomposting soil samples, changes in nutrient content such as Nitrogen (N), Phosphorus (P), and Potassium (K) can be evaluated.

Materials and Reagents/Equipment Required

Organic waste (e.g. kitchen waste, farm residues), Earthworms (Eisenia fetida), Vermicomposting bin or pit, pH meter, Electrical Conductivity (EC) meter, Sieves (2 mm), Balance (digital/analytical), Incubator (if microbial analysis is included), Glassware: beakers, flasks, pipettes, Reagents for NPK analysis (e.g., Kjeldahl reagents, Olsen's reagent, Flame photometer standards).

Procedure

1. **Setup of Vermicomposting:**
   - Fill the bin with a base layer of dry leaves or coco peat.
   - Add pre-decomposed organic waste.
   - Introduce earthworms (~10–15 per kg of waste).
   - Maintain moisture (~60–70%) and cover with jute cloth.
2. **Maintenance:**
   - Maintain temperature (20–30°C).
   - Moisture should be regularly checked and maintained.
   - Mix the compost every 7–10 days to provide aeration.
3. **Harvesting:**
   - After 45–60 days, mature vermicompost is dark, odour-free, and granular.
   - Separate earthworms by light exposure or sieving.
4. **Soil Analysis (Pre and Post Vermicomposting):**
   - Collect soil samples before and after vermicompost application.
   - Analyse pH, EC, and macronutrients (N, P, K) using standard protocols:
     - **Nitrogen** – Kjeldahl method
     - **Phosphorus** – Olsen's method
     - **Potassium** – Flame photometry

Sample Observation Table

Parameter	Before Vermicomposting	After Vermicomposting
pH		
EC (dS/m)		
Available N (%)		
Available P (%)		
Available K (%)		

Precautions

- Use only pre-decomposed or semi-dry waste to prevent worm mortality.
- Avoid adding citrus peels, oily substances, meat, or dairy products.
- Do not allow direct sunlight or heavy rainfall on the compost pit.
- Ensure proper aeration to avoid anaerobic conditions.
- Handle acids and reagents carefully with appropriate PPE during chemical analysis.

Experiment 18

Soil Fauna Survey – Collection and Identification of Earthworms and Insects

Principle

Soil fauna, particularly macrofauna such as earthworms and insects, play a critical role in maintaining soil health, structure, aeration, and nutrient cycling. Surveying soil fauna helps understand biodiversity, ecosystem functions, and the impact of management practices. Identification of these organisms provides insights into soil quality and biological indicators of soil health.

Materials and Reagents/Equipment Required

Hand trowel or soil auger, Polythene bags or sampling containers, Mustard solution (for earthworm extraction, optional), Sieves and forceps, White trays or Petri dishes, Dissecting microscope/Hand lens, Preservative (70% ethanol or isopropyl alcohol), Field notebook and marker, Gloves, spatula, labels.

Procedure

1. **Site Selection and Plot Marking:**
   - Select a representative site (e.g., agricultural field, forest, garden).
   - Mark a 1 m^2 quadrat using a measuring tape and sticks.

2. **Collection of Soil Macrofauna:**
   - Carefully remove soil up to a depth of 15–20 cm.
   - Manually sort the soil and collect visible earthworms and insects into a white tray.
   - Alternatively, for earthworms:
     - Pour mustard solution (50 g powdered mustard in 1 L water) over the soil within the quadrat.
     - Earthworms will surface in 2–5 minutes.

3. **Preservation:**
   - Transfer collected specimens to labelled containers with 70% ethanol.

4. **Identification:**
   - Use taxonomic keys to identify organisms up to family or genus level.
   - Record morphological features using a hand lens or stereo microscope.

5. **Data Recording:**
   - Count and note the number of each type of organism collected per quadrat.

Sample Observation Table

Organism Type	**Number Collected**	**Habitat Notes**	**Identified As (Common/Scientific Name)**
Earthworm		Moist loam soil	*Lumbricus terrestris*
Beetle (adult)		Near decomposing leaves	Carabidae
Ant		Surface layer	Formicidae
Grub or larva		10 cm depth	Scarabaeidae (larvae)

Precautions

- Avoid sampling after rainfall, which may interfere with fauna activity.
- Handle organisms gently to avoid damage.
- Label specimens immediately upon collection.
- Clean all tools before and after use to avoid contamination.
- Avoid prolonged exposure to direct sunlight during sampling.

Experiment 19

Impact of Soil Moisture and pH on Soil Fauna

Principle

Soil fauna, such as earthworms and insects, are sensitive indicators of soil conditions. Their abundance, diversity, and activity are greatly influenced by soil pH and moisture levels. Moisture facilitates mobility and respiration, while pH influences microbial activity and nutrient availability—both directly affecting soil fauna populations. Studying these relationships helps in assessing soil health and ecological balance.

Materials and Reagents/Equipment Required

Soil auger or trowel, pH meter or pH paper, Gravimetric setup or soil moisture probe, Petri dishes or trays, Forceps and hand lens, Preservative (e.g., 70% ethanol), Gloves and labelling materials, Data recording sheets, Field notebook, Earthworm extraction tools (optional: mustard solution).

Procedure

1. **Site Selection and Sampling:**
   - Choose 2–3 sites with varying moisture levels (e.g., dry, moist, waterlogged) and soil types.
   - At each site, mark a 1 m^2 quadrat and collect soil samples up to 15–20 cm depth.
2. **Measurement of Soil Moisture:**
   - Weigh a fresh soil sample.
   - Dry in an oven at 105°C for 24 hours.
   - Calculate moisture content using:

$$\text{Moisture (\%)} = \frac{\text{Fresh weight} - \text{Dry weight}}{\text{Dry weight}} \times 100$$

3. **Measurement of Soil pH:**
   - Prepare a 1:2.5 soil-to-water suspension.
   - Stir and let settle for 30 minutes.
   - Measure pH using a calibrated pH meter or indicator paper.
4. **Soil Fauna Collection:**
   - Manually sort soil for visible fauna or use mustard extraction for earthworms.
   - Count and preserve the collected specimens.
   - Identify fauna under a hand lens or microscope using field guides.
5. **Correlation Analysis:**

- Compare the number and diversity of soil fauna with moisture and pH values from each site.

Sample Observation Table

Site	Soil pH	Moisture (%)	Earthworms Count	Insects Count	Remarks
A	5.8	12	4	3	Slightly acidic, dry soil
B	6.5	18	10	6	Neutral, optimum moisture
C	7.2	30	2	1	Alkaline, waterlogged soil

Precautions

- Avoid disturbing fauna during collection.
- Calibrate pH meter properly before use.
- Ensure soil samples for moisture analysis are weighed immediately.
- Conduct sampling during early morning or evening for active fauna.
- Use gloves and maintain sample hygiene.

Module 4

Soil & Environmental Interactions

Experiment 20

Determination of Heavy Metals in Soil (Using Atomic Absorption Spectrophotometry or Colorimetric Methods)

Principle

Heavy metals such as lead (Pb), cadmium (Cd), chromium (Cr), and zinc (Zn) can accumulate in soil due to industrial activities, agrochemicals, and atmospheric deposition. These elements, even in trace concentrations, can pose serious environmental and health hazards. Atomic Absorption Spectrophotometry (AAS) is a sensitive and widely used method for detecting and quantifying metal concentrations in soil after proper extraction and digestion.

Materials and Reagents/Equipment Required

Soil samples (air-dried and sieved), Conical flasks and funnels, Filter paper (Whatman No. 42), Hot plate or digestion unit, Analytical balance, Volumetric flasks, Atomic Absorption Spectrophotometer (AAS). Standard metal solutions (Pb, Cd, Cr, Zn etc.), Reagents for digestion (e.g., HNO_3, HCl, H_2SO_4), Distilled water, Personal protective equipment (PPE).

Procedure

1. **Sample Preparation:**
   - Air-dry and sieve the soil sample (2 mm mesh).
   - Weigh 1 g of soil and transfer it to a digestion flask.
2. **Soil Digestion:**
   - Add 10 mL of concentrated nitric acid (HNO_3) and heat on a hot plate until white fumes appear.
   - Cool and add 5 mL of perchloric acid ($HClO_4$) or hydrochloric acid (HCl) depending on protocol.
   - Continue heating until the solution becomes clear.
3. **Filtration and Dilution:**
   - Filter the digested sample into a 50 mL volumetric flask.
   - Make up the volume with distilled water.
4. **Instrument Calibration:**
   - Prepare standard solutions of each metal in known concentrations.
   - Calibrate the AAS using blank and standard solutions.
5. **Sample Analysis:**
   - Aspirate the sample into the AAS.
   - Record absorbance for each target metal.

- Calculate the concentration using the calibration curve.

6. **Alternative Colorimetric Method (for simpler labs):**

    - Use appropriate reagents for colour development specific to the metal (e.g., dithizone for Pb).
    - Measure absorbance using a spectrophotometer at the metal-specific wavelength.

Sample Observation Table

Sample ID	Pb (mg/kg)	Cd (mg/kg)	Cr (mg/kg)	Zn (mg/kg)	Remarks
A	23.4	0.45	35.2	56.7	Near roadside area
B	10.2	0.12	12.3	34.1	Agricultural land

Precautions

- Use appropriate PPE when handling acids and metal standards.
- Digest samples in a fume hood.
- Ensure proper calibration of the AAS before analysis.
- Handle glassware carefully to avoid contamination.
- Dispose of heavy metal waste according to environmental safety protocols.

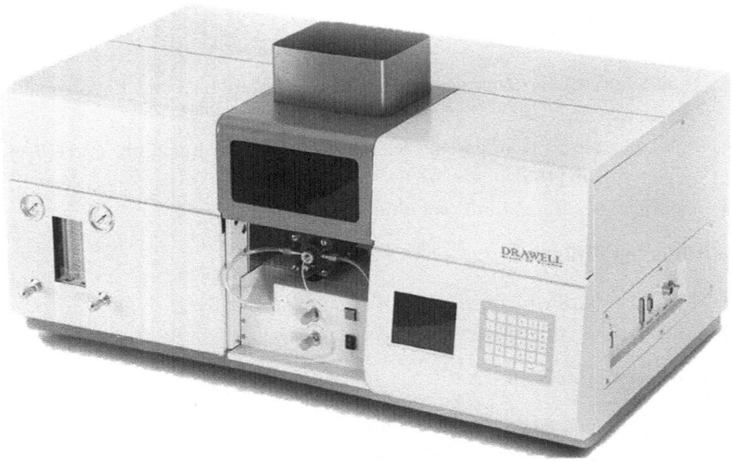

Atomic Absorption Spectrophotometer

Experiment 21

Soil Pollution Index and Environmental Impact Assessment

Principle

The *Soil Pollution Index* (SPI) is a tool used to quantify the level of soil contamination by comparing measured concentrations of pollutants (such as heavy metals or chemicals) against standard permissible limits. Environmental Impact Assessment (EIA) involves systematic analysis to determine the potential effects of pollutants on soil quality and ecosystem health, offering a scientific basis for remediation and land management decisions.

Materials and Reagents/Equipment Required

Soil samples (collected from different locations – agricultural, industrial, residential), Analytical balance, Extraction reagents (e.g., nitric acid, hydrochloric acid), Filtration setup (funnel, filter paper), Atomic Absorption Spectrophotometer (AAS) or colorimeter, Standard solutions of target pollutants (e.g., Pb, Cd, Zn), Distilled water, Measuring cylinders, volumetric flasks, Maps or GPS (for site referencing), Computer with spreadsheet or GIS software (optional).

Procedure

1. **Sample Collection:**
   - Collect composite soil samples from selected locations using a clean auger at 0–15 cm depth.
   - Label and record the GPS location or map reference of each site.
2. **Sample Preparation:**
   - Air-dry and sieve samples (2 mm mesh)
   - Weigh 1 g of each sample for digestion.
3. **Pollutant Extraction and Analysis:**
   - Digest soil samples using concentrated HNO_3 and HCl on a hot plate.
   - Filter and dilute the digested solution.
   - Analyse for heavy metals using AAS or a suitable spectrophotometric method.
4. **Calculation of SPI:**
   - Use the formula:

$$SPN = \frac{1}{n}\sum_{i=1}^{n}\frac{Ci}{Si}$$

Where:

- C_i = Measured concentration of pollutant *i*
- S_i = Standard permissible limit for pollutant *i*
- n = Number of pollutants considered

5. **Environmental Impact Assessment:**

- Interpret SPI values:
    - SPI < 1: Low pollution
    - 1 ≤ SPI ≤ 2: Moderate pollution
    - SPI > 2: High pollution
- Discuss the source of contamination and its potential ecological impacts.

Sample Observation Table

Sample ID	Pb (mg/kg)	Cd (mg/kg)	Zn (mg/kg)	SPI Value	Pollution Level
A	20	0.4	50	0.87	Low pollution
B	60	1.2	150	2.23	High pollution

Standard Limits used: Pb = 50 mg/kg, Cd = 0.5 mg/kg, Zn = 100 mg/kg

Precautions

- Use proper PPE while handling chemical reagents and contaminated soils.
- Avoid cross-contamination between samples.
- Ensure accurate weighing and calibration of instruments.
- Perform the digestion in a fume hood.
- Use appropriate disposal methods for toxic residues.

Experiment 22

Effect of Pesticide Residues on Soil Microbial Populations

Principle

Pesticide residues in soil can alter microbial population dynamics, inhibiting or promoting specific groups such as bacteria, fungi, and actinomycetes. Evaluating these changes helps in understanding the ecological impact of agrochemicals and their long-term implications on soil fertility, microbial biodiversity, and soil health. The serial dilution and plate count method is widely used to assess the effect quantitatively.

Materials and Reagents/Equipment Required

Soil samples from treated (pesticide-applied) and untreated (control) fields, Sterile Petri plates, Nutrient agar (for bacteria), Potato Dextrose Agar (PDA) (for fungi), Actinomycete Isolation Agar (AIA) (for actinomycetes), Sterile distilled water, Autoclave, Laminar flow hood, Incubator, Inoculating loop or pipettes, Sterile test tubes and dilution blanks, Marker pens, notebook.

Procedure

1. **Soil Sample Collection:**
    - Collect composite soil samples from pesticide-treated and untreated areas.
    - Store samples in sterile containers at 4°C until analysis.
2. **Soil Dilution:**
    - Take 1 g of soil and mix with 9 mL of sterile distilled water (10^{-1} dilution).
    - Perform serial dilutions up to 10^{-5}.
3. **Plating:**
    - Plate 0.1 mL from appropriate dilutions onto:
        - Nutrient agar for bacteria
        - PDA (with antibiotics) for fungi
        - AIA for actinomycetes
    - Spread evenly using a sterile spreader.
4. **Incubation:**

- Incubate –
    - Bacteria: 28–30°C for 24–48 hrs
    - Fungi: 25°C for 3–5 days
    - Actinomycetes: 28°C for 5–7 days

5. **Colony Counting:**

- Count colonies and express as colony forming units per gram (CFU/g) of soil.

6. **Comparison:**

   Compare microbial populations between treated and untreated soils to assess pesticide effects.

Sample Observation Table

Sample	Bacteria (CFU/g)	Fungi (CFU/g)	Actinomycetes (CFU/g)	Remarks
Control Soil	2.8×10^6	1.1×10^5	1.5×10^5	Normal population
Treated Soil	1.2×10^6	0.6×10^5	0.8×10^5	Population suppressed

Precautions

- Use aseptic techniques to prevent contamination.
- Autoclave all media and tools before use.
- Avoid exposure of media to air for too long.
- Keep temperature and incubation time consistent.
- Label Petri dishes clearly and incubate inverted to avoid condensation.

Experiment 23

Soil Carbon Sequestration Potential and Organic Carbon Estimation

Principle

Soil acts as a major sink for atmospheric carbon through the sequestration of organic carbon derived from plant residues, root exudates, and microbial biomass. The potential of soil to sequester carbon can be evaluated by estimating soil organic carbon (SOC). One widely used method is the Walkley-Black wet oxidation method, which measures the amount of organic carbon oxidised by potassium dichromate in the presence of sulfuric acid.

Materials and Reagents/Equipment Required

Air-dried and sieved soil samples, 1 N Potassium dichromate ($K_2Cr_2O_7$), Concentrated sulfuric acid (H_2SO_4), Ferrous ammonium sulfate (FAS) – 0.5 N, Diphenylamine indicator or ferroin indicator, Distilled water, Conical flasks, Pipettes and burettes, Measuring cylinders, Titration stand and clamps, Analytical balance, Fume hood and safety gear (gloves, goggles).

Procedure

1. **Sample Preparation:**
   - Weigh 1 g of finely ground, air-dried soil into a 500 mL conical flask.
2. **Oxidation Reaction:**
   - Add 10 mL of 1 N $K_2Cr_2O_7$ solution.
   - Carefully add 20 mL of concentrated H_2SO_4 and swirl gently.
   - Let the mixture stand for 30 minutes under a fume hood.
3. **Dilution and Titration:**
   - Add 200 mL of distilled water to the flask.
   - Add 1–2 drops of diphenylamine indicator
   - Titrate the solution with 0.5 N ferrous ammonium sulfate (FAS) until the colour changes from violet-blue to green.
4. **Blank Titration:**
   - Perform a blank without soil to determine the total oxidising capacity of the dichromate.
5. **Calculation:**
   - % Organic Carbon = $[(B - S) \times N \times 0.003 \times 100] / W$

Where :

B = Volume of FAS used in blank
S = Volume of FAS used in sample
N = Normality of FAS
W = Weight of soil (g)

To estimate **Soil Carbon Sequestration Potential**, use SOC data over time or from treatments such as biochar, compost, or cover crops, considering depth and bulk density.

Sample Observation Table

Sample ID	FAS Volume (Blank) (mL)	FAS Volume (Sample) (mL)	% Organic Carbon	Remarks
A1	25.0	15.2	1.73	Moderate SOC
B2	25.0	18.5	0.96	Low SOC

Precautions

- Always handle concentrated acids under a fume hood using PPE.
- Add acid slowly to avoid splashing and heat generation.
- Ensure accurate titration for precise estimation.
- Calibrate pipettes and burettes before use.
- Dispose of chemical waste responsibly.

Experiment 24

Biochar Preparation and Its Effect on Soil Properties

Principle

Biochar is a stable, carbon-rich product obtained from the pyrolysis of organic biomass under limited oxygen conditions. It enhances soil properties such as pH, water-holding capacity, nutrient availability, and microbial activity. This experiment focuses on preparing biochar using agricultural waste and evaluating its influence on key soil characteristics.

Materials and Reagents/Equipment Required

For Biochar Preparation:

Agricultural biomass (e.g. kitchen waste, crop residues, dal weed, sawdust), Small-scale pyrolysis unit or muffle furnace, Heat-resistant gloves and tongs, Crucibles or metal containers with lids, Pyrolyzer, Thermometer.

For Soil Analysis:

Biochar (crushed and sieved), Soil samples (air-dried and sieved), pH meter, EC meter, Water retention setup, Kjeldahl apparatus or distillation setup (optional for NPK estimation), Soil incubation containers, Analytical balance, Distilled water.

Procedure

A. Biochar Preparation:

- Air-dry the selected biomass.
- Place it in a sealed metal container with limited air entry (to create an oxygen-limited environment) or in a pyrolyzer.
- Heat the container in a furnace at 350–500°C for 2–4 hours.
- Allow the container to cool completely before opening.
- Crush and sieve the resulting black carbonaceous residue to obtain uniform biochar.

Biochar reacy for soil application

B. Application and Soil Property Analysis:

- Mix biochar with soil at different rates (e.g., 0%, 2%, 5% by weight).
- Incubate the mixtures for 1–4 weeks under ambient moisture and temperature conditions.
- After incubation, analyse the following:

- Soil pH using a pH meter (soil: water ratio 1:2.5)
- Electrical Conductivity (EC) using an EC meter
- Water-holding capacity by gravimetric method
- (Optional) Available NPK by standard soil testing procedures

Sample Observation Table

Treatment	**pH**	**EC (dS/m)**	**WHC (%)**	**Comments**
Control	6.2	0.18	35	Baseline
2% Biochar	6.8	0.25	42	Slight improvement
5% Biochar	7.3	0.30	50	Significant improvement

Precautions

- Ensure complete pyrolysis and avoid combustion (no open flames).
- Always allow the furnace/container to cool before opening to avoid fire hazard.
- Use gloves while handling hot equipment or materials.
- Crush and sieve biochar before application for uniform mixing.
- Maintain moisture conditions during incubation for accurate results.

Experiment 25

Soil Degradation and Remediation Techniques (Simulation)

Principle

Soil degradation refers to the decline in soil quality caused by human activities and natural processes, leading to reduced agricultural productivity, erosion, salinisation, contamination, and loss of biodiversity. Remediation techniques aim to restore soil health through physical, chemical, and biological interventions. This simulation-based experiment demonstrates types of soil degradation and evaluates various remediation methods on degraded soil samples.

Materials and Reagents/Equipment Required

For Simulation of Degradation:

Soil samples, Sodium chloride (for salinity), Acid (e.g. dilute HCl for acidification), Organic waste or oil (for contamination), Plastic trays or pots, Watering cans or sprayers.

For Remediation Treatments:

Lime (for acidic soil), Gypsum (for saline-sodic soil), Biochar or compost (organic amendment), Earthworms (optional for biological remediation), pH and EC meters, Weighing balance, Gloves and safety goggles.

Procedure

A. Soil Degradation Simulation:

- Take equal quantities of soil in 4 trays.
- Treat as follows:
  - Tray 1 (Control): No treatment
  - Tray 2: Add excess NaCl to simulate salinity
  - Tray 3: Add dilute HCl to simulate acidification
  - Tray 4: Mix oil or organic waste to simulate contamination
- Allow soils to settle for 3–5 days with mild watering to stabilise the conditions.

B. Remediation:

- Apply the following treatments:
  - Lime to acidic soil
  - Gypsum to saline soil
  - Compost/biochar to contaminated soil
- Monitor the changes in soil pH, EC, and physical appearance over 1–2 weeks.
- Optional: Grow a test plant (e.g. radish) in each tray to evaluate recovery and plant health.

Sample Observation Table

Tray	**Degradation Type**	**pH (Before)**	**pH (After)**	**EC (dS/m) Before**	**EC (dS/m) After**	**Remediation Applied**
1	Control	6.5	6.5	0.20	0.21	None
2	Salinity	6.6	6.8	1.80	0.80	Gypsum
3	Acidification	4.5	6.4	0.25	0.30	Lime
4	Contamination	6.2	6.7	0.35	0.29	Compost + Biochar

Precautions

- Use appropriate safety gear when handling acids, salts, or contaminated materials.
- Avoid over-application of amendments—follow standard rates.
- Keep all trays properly labelled.
- Dispose of contaminated soil responsibly after the experiment.
- Wash hands and equipment thoroughly after the activity.

Module 5

Field & Analytical Techniques

Experiment 26

Soil Sampling for Laboratory Analysis (Using Soil Auger)

Principle

Soil sampling is the process of collecting a soil sample from a specific area of interest to determine the soil's physical, chemical, and biological properties. A soil auger is a common tool used for soil sampling, as it allows for the collection of undisturbed soil from various depths, providing an accurate representation of the soil's profile. The results of soil analysis can provide valuable information for soil fertility, land management, and environmental monitoring.

Materials and Reagents/Equipment Required

Soil auger (manual or powered), Sample bags or containers (clean and labelled), Trowel or spade, GPS or compass (optional for accurate sampling location), Gloves and safety goggles, Soil moisture content meter (optional), Ruler or measuring tape, Paper or plastic sheets (to lay soil samples on), Labels for containers.

Procedure

1. **Preparation of Sampling Site:**
   - Choose a representative location for the soil sample. If the area is large, use a grid system to ensure the sample represents the entire field or region.
   - Ensure that the sampling area is free from contamination (healthy spots) , e.g., avoid areas near roads or high traffic.

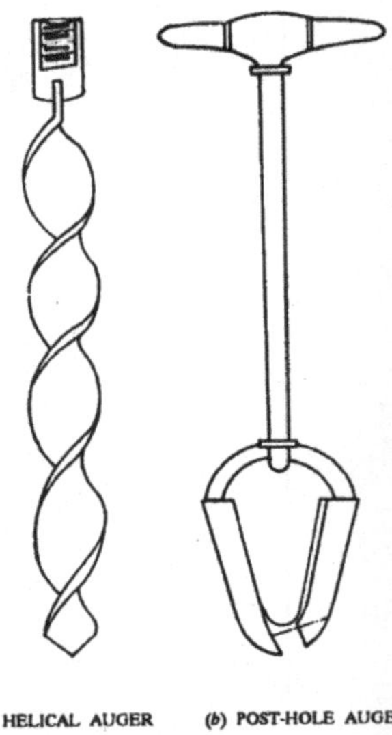

(a) HELICAL AUGER (b) POST-HOLE AUGER

2. **Sampling Procedure:**
   - Wear gloves and safety goggles before starting.
   - Insert the soil auger vertically into the soil to the desired depth. Typically, sampling depths range from 0-15 cm (surface), 15-30 cm, 30-60 cm, and deeper if necessary.
   - Rotate the auger to extract a cylindrical sample of soil.
   - Remove the auger from the hole, and carefully extract the soil sample from the auger into a clean, labelled sample container or bag.
   - If collecting multiple samples from different locations, ensure that each sample is representative of the area and combine them into a composite sample (optional).

3. **Soil Preparation:**
   - Spread the collected soil on a clean paper or plastic sheet.

- Allow it to air dry if necessary (especially for chemical analyses).
- Ensure that no contamination occurs during the drying process.

4. **Storage and Transport:**
    - Seal the sample bags or containers securely, label them with the site, date, depth, and other relevant information.
    - Transport the samples to the laboratory as soon as possible, avoiding extreme temperatures.

Sample Observation Table

Sample No.	**Depth (cm)**	**Location Description**	**Date of Collection**	**Soil Texture**	**Moisture Content (%)**	**Sample Label**
1	0-15	Near field edge	15-02-2025	Loamy	12.5	Sample A1
2	15-30	Near crop rows	15-02-2025	Sandy loam	10.2	Sample B1
3	30-45	Center of field	15-02-2025	Clay	14.7	Sample C1
4	0-15	Near water source	15-02-2025	Silty loam	15.3	Sample D1

Precautions

- Always use clean equipment to avoid contamination between samples.
- Do not take samples from areas with visible contamination such as near roads or trash piles.
- Ensure the auger is properly cleaned between sampling sites to avoid cross-contamination.
- If necessary, take soil samples at multiple points within the sampling area and combine them to form a composite sample.
- Ensure proper labelling and storage of soil samples to maintain traceability and prevent confusion.
- Avoid excessive compaction of the soil sample, which could distort the analysis.

Experiment 27

Preparation of Composite Soil Samples

Principle

A composite soil sample is a mixture of several sub-samples collected from different spots within a defined area to represent the average soil condition of that area. This method helps reduce variability and provides a more accurate analysis of the overall soil health or fertility status. It is particularly useful in agricultural fields, research plots, or environmental monitoring.

Materials and Reagents/Equipment Required

Soil auger or trowel, Clean plastic bucket or tray, Sample collection bags or containers, Labels and permanent marker, Clean plastic sheet (for mixing and drying), Gloves and mask (for safety), Ruler or tape for depth measurement.

Procedure

1. **Select the Sampling Area:**
   - Identify a uniform area (e.g., 1 acre field) based on land use, crop pattern, or topography.
   - Avoid non-representative areas such as near compost pits, roads, water channels, or bunds.
2. **Collection of Sub-samples:**
   - Use a soil auger or trowel to collect soil from at least 10–15 randomly selected healthy spots within the sampling area.
   - Collect soil at the standard root zone depth (usually 0–15 cm for surface soil).
   - Ensure all tools used are clean and dry to avoid contamination.
3. **Preparation of Composite Sample:**
   - Place all sub-samples into a clean plastic bucket or tray.
   - Mix thoroughly to obtain a uniform composite.
   - Remove stones, plant debris, or any other foreign material.

A Trowel

4. **Sample Drying and Storage:**
   - Spread the mixed sample thinly on a clean plastic sheet and allow it to air dry in the shade (not under direct sunlight).

- Once dry, take approximately 500 grams of the mixed sample and store it in a clean, labelled container or sample bag.

5. **Labelling and Recordkeeping:**

   - Label each sample with the following details: sample ID, location, depth, date, and purpose of sampling.

Sample Observation Table

Sub-Sample No.	Depth (cm)	Location Description	Remarks
1	0–15	North-East corner	Normal soil
2	0–15	Near crop rows	Slightly moist
3	0–15	Center of the plot	Good texture
4	0–15	Near irrigation outlet	Avoided (contaminated)
...	...	...	...

Precautions

- Avoid collecting samples when the soil is too wet.
- Use clean tools for every new sampling area.
- Remove organic residues or foreign materials before mixing.
- Ensure the sample is well mixed to truly represent the area.
- Do not expose the sample to direct sunlight or high heat.
- Label all containers clearly to avoid confusion or misplacement.

Experiment 28

GPS-Based Soil Mapping and Surveying

Principle

GPS (*Global Positioning System*)-based soil mapping is a modern geospatial technique used to collect precise location data for soil sampling, survey, and mapping. By integrating GPS with soil data collection, spatial variability in soil properties can be accurately assessed, which helps in site-specific soil management, land use planning, and precision agriculture.

Materials and Reagents/Equipment Required

Handheld GPS device or smartphone with GPS app, Soil auger or trowel, Soil sample collection bags, Field notebook and pen, Base map/topographic map (if available), Computer with GIS software (e.g., QGIS, ArcGIS) for mapping, Measuring tape or rangefinder, Labels and marker.

Procedure

1. **Planning the Survey:**
   - Define the boundaries of the area to be surveyed (e.g., field, watershed, or research plot).
   - Divide the area into a grid or sample units based on the study objective.
2. **Field Data Collection:**
   - Go to each predetermined location and use a GPS device to record the latitude and longitude coordinates.
   - At each location, collect a soil sample using a trowel or auger (as per depth requirement, typically 0–15 cm).
   - Record additional observations such as slope, land use, vegetation cover, or soil colour.
3. **Data Recording:**
   - Note down the coordinates and field data in a notebook or directly in a GPS-linked data logging app.
   - Assign a sample ID to each point and corresponding soil sample.
4. **Post-Survey Processing:**
   - Transfer the recorded GPS coordinates and soil data into a computer.
   - Use GIS software (like QGIS or ArcGIS) to create **soil maps** showing spatial patterns (e.g., pH variation, organic carbon, etc.).
   - Maps can be overlaid with other data such as elevation or land use for integrated interpretation.

Sample Observation Table

Sample ID	Latitude (°N)	Longitude (°E)	Depth (cm)	Observations
S1	34.089152	74.797003	0–15	Slightly acidic soil
S2	34.089982	74.797912	0–15	Sandy texture
S3	34.090605	74.798630	0–15	Near irrigation source

Precautions

- Ensure the GPS device is fully charged before going to the field.
- Collect samples only when weather permits (avoid rainy conditions).
- Record coordinates carefully and verify accuracy at each point.
- Avoid interference from buildings or trees when using GPS.
- Use consistent sampling depth and method across all locations.
- Label soil samples clearly and link them to GPS data accurately.

Experiment 29

Soil Nutrient Analysis Using Spectrophotometer (N, P, K, Fe & Zn)

Principle

Spectrophotometry is a widely used method to quantify nutrient elements in soil extracts by measuring light absorption at specific wavelengths. Soil nutrients such as phosphorus (P), iron (Fe), and zinc (Zn) are usually estimated by forming coloured complexes with specific reagents, and their concentration is deduced from calibration curves. Nitrogen (N) is often determined using colorimetric reactions, and potassium (K) is generally measured via flame photometry but can also be detected colorimetrically using turbidimetric or tetraphenylborate methods.

Materials and Reagents/Equipment Required

UV-Visible Spectrophotometer, Soil samples (air-dried and sieved),

Extraction solutions:

- N: Alkaline $KMnO_4$
- P: Olsen's or Bray's reagent
- K: Neutral normal ammonium acetate
- Fe & Zn: DTPA (Diethylenetriaminepentaacetic acid)

Colour-developing reagents:

- N: Nessler's reagent
- P: Ammonium molybdate and stannous chloride
- Fe: Orthophenanthroline
- Zn: Dithizone

Standard solutions (KH_2PO_4, KCl, $FeSO_4$, $ZnSO_4$, NH_4Cl), Filter papers (Whatman No. 42), Glassware (beakers, pipettes, volumetric flasks), Mechanical shaker, Distilled water, Protective gear (gloves, goggles).

Procedure Overview

A. Available Nitrogen (Alkaline $KMnO_4$ Method)

- Digest soil with alkaline $KMnO_4$ and distil ammonia.
- Trap ammonia in boric acid.
- Titrate with standard acid OR measure colour using Nessler's reagent at 410 nm.

B. Available Phosphorus (Olsen's Method)

- Extract soil with $NaHCO_3$.
- Filter and treat aliquot with ammonium molybdate and stannous chloride.

- Measure absorbance at 660 nm.

C. Available Potassium

- Extract with neutral 1N ammonium acetate.
- Measure colour or turbidity using spectrophotometer at ~720 nm (or flame photometry preferred).

D. Available Iron (Fe)

- Extract with DTPA solution.
- Add orthophenanthroline reagent.
- Read absorbance at 510 nm.

E. Available Zinc (Zn)

- Extract with DTPA.
- Add dithizone reagent.
- Measure absorbance at 535 nm.

Precautions

- Ensure all glassware is clean and contaminant-free.
- Use freshly prepared reagents and standard solutions.
- Calibrate spectrophotometer before measurements.
- Follow proper timing for colour development reactions.
- Use appropriate wavelength settings for each element.

Experiment 30

Interpretation of Soil Test Reports for Fertility Recommendations

Principle

Soil test reports provide quantified data on the availability of essential nutrients and other soil parameters such as pH, electrical conductivity (EC), organic carbon, and micronutrient levels. Interpretation of these values allows for scientific assessment of soil fertility status and helps in making appropriate fertiliser and soil amendment recommendations. This process ensures sustainable nutrient management and enhances crop productivity while minimising environmental damage.

Materials and Tools Required

Soil test reports (actual or simulated), Fertility rating chart for macro- and micronutrients, Soil test interpretation guides (regional/state-wise), Fertiliser recommendation sheets or software (if available), Calculator or spreadsheet software, Pen, notebook, or interpretation sheets, Regional soil fertility and crop requirement data, Extension bulletins or government guidelines (e.g. ICAR, SKUAST-K).

Procedure

1. **Collect a Soil Test Report**
    - Use either a real soil test report from a lab or a prepared sample report. The report should include values for:
        - pH, EC
        - Organic Carbon (%)
        - Available Nitrogen (kg/ha)
        - Available Phosphorus (kg/ha)
        - Available Potassium (kg/ha)
        - Micronutrients (Zn, Fe, Mn, Cu)
2. **Refer to Standard Rating Chart**
    - Use a standard nutrient rating chart to categorise nutrient levels as Low, Medium, or High.

Standard Soil Fertility Rating Chart (as per ICAR guidelines)

Parameter	Low	Medium	High
Organic Carbon (%)	< 0.5	$0.5 – 0.75$	> 0.75

Available Nitrogen (kg/ha)	< 280	280 – 560	> 560
Available Phosphorus (kg/ha) (Olsen's P)	< 10	10 – 25	> 25
Available Potassium (kg/ha)	< 110	110 – 280	> 280
Available Sulphur (ppm)	< 10	10 – 20	> 20
Zinc (Zn) (ppm)	< 0.6	0.6 – 1.2	> 1.2
Iron (Fe) (ppm)	< 4.5	4.5 – 9.0	> 9.0
Manganese (Mn) (ppm)	< 2.0	2.0 – 4.0	> 4.0
Copper (Cu) (ppm)	< 0.2	0.2 – 0.5	> 0.5
Soil pH	< 6.0 (acidic)	6.5 – 7.5 (neutral)	> 8.0 (alkaline)
Electrical Conductivity (dS/m)	< 1.0 (normal)	1.0 – 2.0 (moderate)	> 2.0 (saline)

***Note:** These values are generalised and suitable for most alluvial, red, and loamy soils in India. Some states have slightly modified thresholds for specific regions or crops (e.g., Kashmir Valley soils). Always consult the local State Agricultural University (SKUAST-K) or ICAR bulletin for tailored recommendations.*

3. **Interpret Each Parameter**
   - Check soil pH and EC for acidity/alkalinity or salinity.
   - Use Organic Carbon % to assess organic matter status.
   - Classify macro- and micronutrients using rating charts.
4. **Determine Nutrient Deficiencies or Excesses**
   - Identify any deficient or borderline nutrients.
   - Note any imbalance between nutrients (e.g., high K vs low N).
5. **Make Fertility Recommendations**
   - Suggest suitable fertilisers and application doses based on deficiencies.
   - Suggest soil amendments (e.g., lime for acidic soil, gypsum for sodic soil).
   - Recommend integrated practices like biofertilisers, compost, or green manuring where applicable.
6. **Prepare a Recommendation Report**

- Include a summary of interpretations.
- Include crop-specific fertiliser recommendations.
- Provide sustainable management tips.

Sample Observation Table

Parameter	Value	Interpretation	Recommendation
pH	5.8	Slightly acidic	Apply lime @ 2 t/ha
Organic Carbon (%)	0.42	Medium	Apply FYM @ 5 t/ha
Available N (kg/ha)	240	Low	Apply urea @ 100 kg/ha
Available P (kg/ha)	14	Medium	Apply SSP @ 60 kg/ha
Available K (kg/ha)	125	Medium	Apply MOP @ 30 kg/ha
Zn (ppm)	0.5	Deficient	Apply $ZnSO_4$ @ 25 kg/ha

Precautions

- Always use the correct regional rating chart and crop-specific guidelines.
- Avoid blanket fertiliser recommendations without interpretation.
- Use updated reports not older than 6 months for accuracy.
- Consider previous crop history and expected yield.

Annexure – I

References

Determination of Soil Texture (By Hydrometer and Feel Method)	• Bouyoucos, G. J. (1962). Hydrometer method improved for making particle size analyses of soils 1. *Agronomy journal*, *54*(5), 464-465. • Gee, G. W., & Or, D. (2002). 2.4 Particle-size analysis. *Methods of soil analysis: Part 4 physical methods*, *5*, 255-293. • Nachtergaele, F. (2001). Soil taxonomy—A basic system of soil classification for making and interpreting soil surveys. *Geoderma*, *99*(3-4), 336-337. • Thien, S. J. (1979). A flow diagram for teaching texture-by-feel analysis. *Journal of Agronomic education*, *8*(1), 54-55.
Soil Colour and Its Significance (Using Munsell Soil Colour Chart)	• Weil, R., & Brady, N. (2016). The nature and properties of soils, 15th edn., edited by: Fox, D. *D.[Google Scholar]*. • Chadwick, O. A., Hendricks, D. M., & Nettleton, W. D. (1989). Silicification of holocene soils in northern monitor valley, Nevada. *Soil Science Society of America Journal*, *53*(1), 158-164.
Bulk Density and Particle Density Measurement	• Bandyopadhyay, K., Aggarwal, P., Chakraborty, D., Pradhan, S., Garg, R. N., & Singh, R. (2012). Practical manual on measurement of soil physical properties. *Division of Agricultural Physics, Indian Agricultural Research Institute, New Delhi-110012, India*, *62*. • Brogowski, Z., Kwasowski, W., & Madyniak, R. (2014). Calculating particle density, bulk density, and total porosity of soil based on its texture. *Soil science annual*, *65*(4), 139.
Porosity and Infiltration Rate of Soil	• Danielson, R. E., & Sutherland, P. L. (1986). Porosity. *Methods of soil analysis: part 1 physical and mineralogical methods*, *5*, 443-461.

	• Hillel, D. (1998). *Environmental Soil Physics*. Academic Press. NM Geology & Minerals • Basche, A. D., & DeLonge, M. S. (2019). Comparing infiltration rates in soils managed with conventional and alternative farming methods: A meta-analysis. *PloS one*, *14*(9).
Soil Moisture Content Determination (Gravimetric and Tensiometer Method)	• Gardner, W. H. (1986). Water content. *Methods of soil analysis: Part 1 physical and mineralogical methods*, *5*, 493-544. • Majhi, T., & Sarkar, N. (2019). Study on soil moisture variations in responding to Tensiometer and soil moisture meter with respect to gravimetric method. *International Journal of Chemical Studies*, *7*(4), 3179. • Hillel, D. (1998). Environmental Soil Physics Academic Press. *San Diego, CA*. • Carter, M. R., & Gregorich, E. G. (2007). *Soil sampling and methods of analysis*. CRC press.
Water Holding Capacity of Soil	• Olorunfemi, I., Fasinmirin, J., & Ojo, A. (2016). Modeling cation exchange capacity and soil water holding capacity from basic soil properties. *Eurasian Journal of Soil Science*, *5*(4), 266-274. • Carter, M. R., & Gregorich, E. G. (2007). *Soil sampling and methods of analysis*. CRC press.
Soil pH and Electrical Conductivity (EC) Determination	• Smith, J. L., & Doran, J. W. (1997). Measurement and use of pH and electrical conductivity for soil quality analysis. *Methods for assessing soil quality*, *49*, 169-185. • Tandon, H. L. S. (2005). *Methods of analysis of soils, plants, waters, fertilisers & organic manures*.
Estimation of Organic Carbon (Walkley-Black Method)	• Smith, J. L., & Doran, J. W. (1997). Measurement and use of pH and electrical conductivity for soil quality analysis. *Methods for assessing soil quality*, *49*, 169-185.

	• Tandon, H. L. S. (2005). *Methods of analysis of soils, plants, waters, fertilisers & organic manures* (pp. xi+-203).
Available Nitrogen Estimation (Alkaline $KMnO_4$ Method)	• Subbiah, B. V., & Asija, G. L. (1956). A rapid procedure for the estimation of available nitrogen in soils. • Stanford, G. (1982). Assessment of soil nitrogen availability. *Nitrogen in agricultural soils*, *22*, 651-688
Estimation of Available Phosphorus (Olsen's Method)	• Olsen, S. R. (1954). *Estimation of available phosphorus in soils by extraction with sodium bicarbonate* (No. 939). US Department of Agriculture. • Richardson, A. E., & Simpson, R. J. (2011). Soil microorganisms mediating phosphorus availability update on microbial phosphorus. *Plant physiology*, *156*(3), 989-996.
Available Potassium Determination (Flame Photometry)	• Jackson, M. L. (1973). *Soil chemical analysis*. Prentice Hall of India Pvt. Ltd. • Van Diest, A. (1978). Factors affecting the availability of potassium in soils. *Iiunm*, 37.
Cation Exchange Capacity (CEC) Measurement	• Jackson, M. (1958). Soil chemical analysis prentice Hall. *Inc., Englewood Cliffs, NJ*, *498*(1958), 183-204. • Sparks, D. L., Page, A. L., Helmke, P. A., & Loeppert, R. H. (Eds.). (2020). *Methods of soil analysis, part 3: Chemical methods*. John Wiley & Sons.
Soil Fertility Evaluation and Nutrient Deficiency Diagnosis	• Jadeja, A. S., Hirpara, D. V., Vekaria, L. C., & Sakarvadia, H. L. (2021). *Soil fertility and nutrient management: a way to sustainable agriculture*. CRC Press. • Osman, K. T., & Osman, K. T. (2013). Plant nutrients and soil fertility management. *Soils: Principles, properties and management*, 129-159.
Microbial Biomass Carbon Estimation	• Vance, E. D., Brookes, P. C., & Jenkinson, D. S. (1987). An extraction method for measuring soil microbial biomass C. *Soil biology and Biochemistry*, *19*(6), 703-707.

	• Joergensen, R. G. (1996). The fumigation-extraction method to estimate soil microbial biomass: calibration of the kEC value. *Soil Biology and Biochemistry*, *28*(1), 25-31.
Soil Respiration Measurement	• Anderson, J. P. (1982). Soil respiration. *Methods of soil analysis: part 2 chemical and microbiological properties*, *9*, 831-871. • Paul, E. A. (2007). Soil microbiology, ecology, and biochemistry in perspective. In *Soil microbiology, ecology and biochemistry* (pp. 3-24). Academic Press. • Subba, R. (2017). *Soil microbiology*. Oxford and IBH publishing.
Vermicomposting and Its Effects on Soil Nutrient Status	• Edwards, C. A., & Arancon, N. Q. (2004). The use of earthworms in the breakdown of organic wastes to produce vermicomposts and animal feed protein. In *Earthworm ecology* (pp. 345-379). CRC press. • Walkley, A., & Black, I. A. (1934). An examination of the Degtjareff method for determining soil organic matter, and a proposed modification of the chromic acid titration method. *Soil science*, *37*(1), 29-38.
Soil Fauna Survey: Collection and Identification of Earthworms and Insects	
Impact of Soil Moisture and pH on Soil Fauna (Entomology Perspective)	• Edwards, C.A., & Bohlen, P.J. (1996). *Biology and Ecology of Earthworms*, Chapman and Hall. • Lavelle, Patrick, and Alister V. Spain. "Soil organisms." *Soil ecology* (2001): 201-356. • Brussaard, L. (1997). Biodiversity and ecosystem functioning in soil. *Ambio*, 563-570. • Anderson, J. M., & Ingram, J. S. (1994). Tropical soil biology and fertility: a handbook of methods. *Soil Science*, *157*(4), 265.
Determination of Heavy Metals in Soil (Using Atomic Absorption Spectrophotometry or Colorimetric Methods)	• Alloway, B. J. (Ed.). (2012). *Heavy metals in soils: trace metals and metalloids in soils*

	and their bioavailability (Vol. 22). Springer Science & Business Media.
Soil Pollution Index and Environmental Impact Assessment	• Sparks, D. L., Page, A. L., Helmke, P. A., & Loeppert, R. H. (Eds.). (2020). *Methods of soil analysis, part 3: Chemical methods*. John Wiley & Sons.
Effect of Pesticide Residues on Soil Microbial Populations	• Arora, S., Arora, S., Sahni, D., Sehgal, M., Srivastava, D. S., & Singh, A. (2019). Pesticides use and its effect on soil bacteria and fungal populations, microbial biomass carbon and enzymatic activity. *Current science*, *116*(4), 643-649. • Rangaswami, G., & Bagyaraj, D. J. (2004). Agricultural microbiology, 6. printing.
Soil Carbon Sequestration Potential and Organic Carbon Estimation	• Nelson, D. W., & Sommers, L. E. (1982). Total carbon, organic carbon, and organic matter. *Methods of soil analysis: Part 2 chemical and microbiological properties*, *9*, 539-579. • Walkley, A., & Black, I. A. (1934). An examination of the Degtjareff method for determining soil organic matter, and a proposed modification of the chromic acid titration method. *Soil science*, *37*(1), 29-38.
Biochar Preparation and Its Effect on Soil Properties	• Chan, K. Y., Van Zwieten, L., Meszaros, I., Downie, A., & Joseph, S. (2007). Agronomic values of green waste biochar as a soil amendment. *Soil Research*, *45*(8), 629-634. • IBI (International Biochar Initiative). (2021). *Biochar Production Guidelines*.
Soil Degradation and Remediation Techniques (Simulation)	• Lal, R. (2015). Restoring soil quality to mitigate soil degradation. *Sustainability*, *7*(5), 5875-5895. • Weil, R., & Brady, N. (2016). The nature and properties of soils, 15th edn., edited by: Fox, D. *D*.
Soil Sampling for Laboratory Analysis (Using Soil Auger)	• Carter, M. R., & Gregorich, E. G. (2007). *Soil sampling and methods of analysis*. CRC press.

Preparation of Composite Soil Samples	• Carter, M. R., & Gregorich, E. G. (2007). *Soil sampling and methods of analysis*. CRC press.
GPS-Based Soil Mapping and Surveying	• Kaliraj, S., Adhikari, K., Dharumarajan, S., Lalitha, M., & Kumar, N. (2024). Remote sensing and geographic information system applications in mapping and assessment of soil resources. In *Remote Sensing of Soils* (pp. 25-41). Elsevier.
Soil Nutrient Analysis Using Spectrophotometer	• Olsen, S. R. (1954). *Estimation of available phosphorus in soils by extraction with sodium bicarbonate* (No. 939). US Department of Agriculture. • Tandon, H. L. S. (2005). *Methods of analysis of soils, plants, waters, fertilisers & organic manures*. • Lindsay, W. L., & Norvell, W. (1978). Development of a DTPA soil test for zinc, iron, manganese, and copper. *Soil science society of America journal*, *42*(3), 421-428. • Subbiah, B. V., & Asija, G. L. (1956). A rapid procedure for the estimation of available nitrogen in soils.
Interpretation of Soil Test Reports for Fertility Recommendations	• ICAR (Indian Council of Agricultural Research) Soil Health Card Scheme Guidelines.

Annexure – II

Common Conversion Relationships

Parameter	Conversion	Relationship
Area	hectares ↔ square meters	1 ha = 10,000 m^2
	acres ↔ hectares	1 acre = 0.4047 ha
Weight	tonnes ↔ kilograms	1 tonne = 1000 kg
Volume	cubic meters ↔ litres	1 m^3 = 1000 L
Soil Bulk Density	g/cm^3 ↔ kg/m^3	1 g/cm^3 = 1000 kg/m^3
Concentration	ppm ↔ mg/kg (in soil)	1 ppm = 1 mg/kg
	ppm ↔ mg/L (in solution)	1 ppm ≈ 1 mg/L (for dilute aqueous solutions)
Electrical Conductivity (EC)	dS/m ↔ mmhos/cm	1 dS/m = 1 mmhos/cm
	dS/m ↔ µS/cm	1 dS/m = 1000 µS/cm
Pressure	atm ↔ kPa	1 atm = 101.325 kPa
	bar ↔ kPa	1 bar = 100 kPa
Nitrogen (N)	N% ↔ N kg/ha	N% × 10000 = N kg/ha (for 1 ha of soil to 15 cm depth)
pH	pH unit ↔ H^+ concentration	$pH = -\log_{10}[H^+]$
Carbon to Organic Matter	Organic C ↔ Organic Matter	Organic Matter ≈ Organic C × 1.724
CEC	meq/100g ↔ cmol(+)/kg	1 meq/100g = 1 cmol(+)/kg
Temperature	°C ↔ K	K = °C + 273.15